*A Book
about Dying*

A Book about Dying

Preparing for Eternal Life

~

Robert H. Kirven

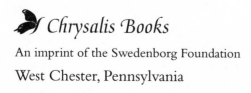
Chrysalis Books

An imprint of the Swedenborg Foundation

West Chester, Pennsylvania

Library of Congress Cataloging-in-Publication Data:

Kirven, Robert H.
    A book about dying : preparing for eternal life / by Robert H. Kirven.
        p.   cm.
    ISBN 0-87785-175-1
    1. Death—Religious aspects—New Jerusalem Church.   2. Swedenborg,
    Emanuel, 1688-1722.   3. New Jerusalem Church—Doctrines.   I.
    Title.
    BX8729.D35K57   1997
    236'. 1—dc21   96—40850
                                                                              CIP

Edited by Mary Lou Bertucci
Designed by Vivian L. Bradbury
Cover art: *Red Poppies*, Charles DeMuth. The Metropolitan Museum of Art, Gift of Henry and Louise Loeb, 1983. (1983.40) © 1983 The Metropolitan Museum of Art, New York.
Typeset in Bembo by Sans Serif, Inc.

Chrysalis Books is an imprint of the Swedenborg Foundation, Inc. For information contact:
    Chrysalis Books
    Swedenborg Foundation
    320 North Church Street
    West Chester, Pennsylvania 19380

Contents ∽

Contents

Contents

Foreword ~

by Simcha Paull Raphael, Ph.D.

There is a story told about a great holy man who was close to the last moments of his life. As he lay in bed, his grief-stricken wife burst into tears. With equanimity, the dying man looked at her lovingly, and said, "Why are you crying? My whole life was only that I might learn how to die." With these words, he died peacefully, fully accepting his finite human fate.

Whenever I think about this deathbed scene, I ask myself what it would mean to spend one's whole life learning how to die. It's not an idea we think about very often. Prescriptions for life, not death, are taught by parents and promulgated in schools. From a young age, children are given life skills; adolescents are taught how to cope with the vicissitudes of social and economic life in our times; and elders are given inspirational guidelines to keep on living, enjoying life. As a society, we do all we can to avoid the topic of death—and yet, as human beings, we must die. So how can we learn to die, and even more, learn to live well so that we may die well? Who will be our teachers? Where can we find the wisdom necessary to help us in preparing to meet our death, whenever that might take place?

It is exactly this task Robert Kirven has taken on in writing *A Book about Dying: Preparing for Eternal Life*. As a scholar of religious thought and an authority on Emanuel Swedenborg, Kirven walks us through a compassionate approach to meeting death. Weaving the visionary insights found in Swedenborg's theological writings with his own experience before and since the death of his wife, Marian, he provides a simple and yet profound message. Death is not the end of human existence, but only a transition to another realm of consciousness—and the way in which we live has profound impact upon the destiny that awaits us at the moment of death and in the world beyond.

In my own personal and professional life, I have given much time reflecting on death and its impact on human beings. Besides working as a grief therapist, I teach helping professionals and clergy how to counsel the dying and bereaved. I have also studied what many of the great religious traditions of the world have to say about immortality and the journey of the soul. In addition, I have written a book *Jewish Views of the Afterlife* (1994). So when I encountered this work, I was delighted to discover the clear guidelines the author has delineated for learning how to die and how to live, accepting the inevitability of death with integrity and wisdom.

Given the reality of mortality, people often ask questions about life after death. Is there an eternal soul? Is there consciousness beyond the grave? What happens after physical death to the person that I think I am while I am still alive? In wrestling with such questions about death and the afterlife, we need maps, models, and guidelines. If I am going to drive from New York to San Francisco, I call my local motor club and request road maps because I find it helpful to familiarize myself with the freeways, turnpikes, and other routes I will follow. Robert Kirven has done for life after death what motor clubs do for interstate travel: he provides a comprehensive cartography of the realms of consciousness one encounters after physical death.

Death, notes the author, is only the termination of the

body/spirit union; subsequently, reality of another order en-
sues. After bodily death, one gracefully enters a supernal
spiritual existence populated with luminescent angelic beings, old souls, beloved friends and family members. One
lives in a state of disembodied awareness, transcending the
usual limits of time, space, and geography. Dynamic and
everchanging, this spiritual world after death—what Kirven
calls "living after dying"—reflects the level of spiritual development one has attained during embodied life. Thus, to
know the cartography of the world beyond well in advance
of death makes for a more peaceful and radiant journey.
Since many great philosophers and mystics have seen into
the invisible worlds of immortal life, among them Emanuel
Swedenborg, we can learn from the wisdom they have
passed on.

Once we become familiar with the cartography of the
world beyond physical mortality, then what? What are the
implications of understanding the spiritual terrain of the
soul's journey?

A Book about Dying provides not only a map of the afterlife journey, but also action directives *in this life* for dying
with dignity and spiritual awareness. In the face of death,
people often feel alone and afraid. Family members feel
helpless and disempowered in an overwhelming, high-tech
medical environment. Approaching the end of life in a hospital bed, surrounded by tubes, electronic monitoring de-
vices, and overworked medical personnel, is not the ideal
situation for an experience of spiritually awakened dying.
But given increasing life expectancy and the environment of
most hospitals and nursing homes, this is the reality we may
well encounter with the deaths of loved ones and with our
own death.

The spiritual teachings outlined in this book remind us

that death is a process of transformation. Undoubtedly, in terminal illness there can be excruciating physical pain for the dying person and deep emotional stress for loved ones. But at another level, the process of dying prepares a soul to leave behind the physical form. If we embrace the truth of the life of the spirit, we can recognize that death is only death of the body and, simultaneously, is an opening to a new creation beyond all the agonies and distress of physical life. Utilizing this awareness as a basis for dealing with the dying, family members and professional caregivers will be empowered to assist a person at the time of death. We can be active participants in aiding souls as they transit this world into the next. With an open heart, a clear mind, and an intuitive spirit, we can learn to attune to the soul, or consciousness, of a person who is dying. At a nonverbal level, within the subtle planes of mind where souls inter-connect, we can help a dying person surrender the attach-ments of this world, and gently awaken to the life beyond. We are being asked nothing less than to become soul guides for each other at the moment of death. In this book, we are given wise counsel enabling us to embark upon this holy task.

Finally, the words of this book will provide great solace for the bereaved. From my own life and from stories I have been privileged to share with clients, I know how deeply painful grief and loss can be. To lose a loved one—be it a parent, spouse, sibling, child, or friend—can be one of the most lonely and heartbreaking experiences in life. In death, a relationship between two human beings feels drastically severed, ended completely. This sense of radical disconnec-tion is often reinforced by our cultural milieu. The influ-ence of scientific materialism has ingrained within our culture the idea that, once dead, the person is gone forever.

Pull the plug: the life systems cease. There is only silence and a wall, no further communication between the deceased and surviving loved ones. The sense of being cut off from loved ones is exacerbated by the discomfort people often feel around those in mourning. Even well-meaning friends and family rapidly grow tired of listening to the bereaved speak about their loved ones. We prefer to hear people say they are doing fine in the face of grief. So bereaved people frequently live through a protracted period of isolation, bearing as unobtrusively as possible the lonely, painful burden of grief.

However, teachings on life after death, throughout history and across the planet, have always asserted that there exists a thread of interconnection between the living and the dead. If death is nothing more than a transition to another realm, then there is conscious awareness after death; and the prospect exists for continued communication between this world and the world beyond. Between the worlds of the living and of the dead, there is a window, not a wall, that can be opened in sacred moments through a variety of means, including but not limited to rituals of memorialization, prayer, meditation, visions, or dreams. We can know unequivocally that the heart and mind of the bereaved and the soul of deceased can—and do—find moments for contact and communication.

The bond between human beings transcends physical mortality. As we grow spiritually, we can live increasingly with a conscious awareness of that divine realm where our loved ones abide. By opening the window to the invisible world, we can transform alienation and loneliness into a sense of connection with spirit beings who are no longer in the world of the living. Infusing this spiritual perspective into our experience of bereavement will transform mourning into meaning, heal the hurting heart, and awaken the individual soul to the deeper mysteries of life and death. This book makes a wonderful contribution to the growing body of literature on spiritual perspectives on dying and death. It is a manual for conscious living and dying.

Department of Religion
LaSalle University
Philadelphia, Pennsylvania

Introduction ∿

This book about dying started out in my mind to be a fresh presentation of material I had studied and taught to graduate students preparing for ordination, during my three decades on the faculty of the Swedenborg School of Religion. I had long thought that the subject needed development to make it more accessible to individuals facing the challenges of death—their own impending death or the death of a loved one—and for those who are ready to look at their own life in the light of their eventual death and their life after death.

The project felt personally relevant, too. For four or five years I had been caretaker for my wife Marian, in what I expected to be a terminal illness—although I did not foresee her dying within the next few years. However, my progress on the manuscript fell into a kind of synchronicity with the progress of her disease, and I found myself writing about what I was experiencing. Since her dying was so much a part of my living while I was writing this book, it feels important to me that something about her be told here.

More than fifty years ago, I had literally bumped into Marian on a trolley car on which we were both going to the University of Chicago (Judy Garland's "The Trolley Song" was on *The Hit Parade* at the time). In the half century since, we became partners in marriage and raising two daughters, in graduate education, and many aspects of my career. She was a determinedly active person, with a quick sense of humor, quietly held but unshakable convictions, and little concern for status or appearances; but with such a love for people, animals, and even plants that she sometimes wept when pruning and put out food for field mice that invaded our basement in the winter. When our denomination began ordaining women, she made a preaching gown as a gift for every woman who was graduated from our seminary.

After our two daughters were happily married and caring for their own children, Marian said to a circle of our friends that her life's primary goals had been accomplished and that any more that life brought would be just icing on the cake. A few years later, she retired, after twenty years as librarian at the school where I taught, when she was fifty-nine. That seemed early for retirement, but I have suspected since that some kind of premonition may have prompted her. She trusted her intuition, which was sometimes surprisingly on target. For example, one evening she was playing solitaire while I watched the *NBC Nightly News*; the news anchor John Chancellor said, "You'll be surprised at what [reporter] Fred Briggs was doing with Idi Amin"; Marian (who had known Fred Briggs as a boy) commented quietly, "Probably playing basketball." She was right—just as she had been right on a more serious matter when she talked her mother into entering a retirement community, only months before the onset of her mother's Alzheimer's disease would have made her ineligible for admission.

Within three years of her retirement, occasional symptoms of speech difficulty began to appear, and in another four years Marian was virtually speechless. Her ability to write failed almost as fast, leaving her unable to communicate except by playing a kind of "charades," and the failure gradually spread to other manual skills. Toward the end of her life, she became almost helpless. However, she knew me and her family and neighbors—and kept track of the date and our appointments—until the end. Even while she was dependent on me for most of the day's manual tasks, she initiated and influenced our search for a retirement community, helping me prepare for when she could no longer help me. ✓

At the time I started writing this book, we were living in an apartment in the Glencroft Retirement Community in Glendale, Arizona. Marian required almost full-time care, but the gradual expansion of her needs gave me time to develop the skills I needed to do what had to be done for her. While I was writing the final section of this book, she was hospitalized with a medical emergency that brought her to a comatose state. On two occasions, she appeared close enough to death that I said aloud to her unconscious form, "If you can get better and come home with me, Marian, that will be wonderful; but if you want to let go and die, that's okay. I'll be all right."

Eventually, my daughters and I decided with her physician that we would withhold further medication and wait for the end. Surprisingly, that decision led to her partial recovery (one of the medications may have been part of the problem). After a few weeks she was home under my care again; but in a few months—on the forty-eighth anniversary of our marriage, as it happened—she moved to our on-site nursing facility again.

I had resisted moving her to the care center, expecting her to feel I was abandoning her. However, she took an active interest in the packing for her move and never seemed anxious to get out of the center or disturbed when I left. In fact, after I had been with her awhile on one of my first visits, she led me to where I had left my hat and handed it to me. In the kind of communication that we had developed, she was letting me know I didn't have to worry about her now.

A few days later, I visited her while a pianist was playing hymns for patients in her section, and some of the staff and visitors were singing along. I was sitting beside her, holding her hand and singing, uncertain whether she was listening or dozing, when she surprised me. We were singing "What a friend we have in Jesus / All our pains and griefs to bear / What a privilege to carry / Everything to God in prayer," when Marian looked at me, smiled, and nodded in agreement! A few minutes later, after the pianist had gone, Marian was standing as if she were looking at the floor. Her eyes were closed, and she didn't appear to recognize our daughter Diana's greeting when she arrived to visit. I told Diana what had just happened. With tears in her eyes, she hugged her mother and said, "O, Mom! I forget that even though you can't talk to me, you can still talk to Jesus!" And once again, Marian raised her head, smiled, and nodded her affirmation.

This stay in the nursing home was briefer than we expected. Marian slept or was unconscious more than she was awake. I repeated my "releasing" speech, not knowing if she heard me (practice does not make it perceptibly easier); one day, she quit eating. Just over three weeks after her admission, Marian died peacefully, apparently in her sleep. Diana and the hospice chaplain were at her bedside. At the moment she died, our other daughter, Margaret, who lived twenty-five-hundred miles away, felt a need to talk to her sister. Margaret's call reached Diana at the center's nursing station a few minutes after Marian's death, providing an example of the kind of knowledge I describe in the chapter

"Supporting Characters" that existed between my father and his twin sister.

The synchronicity of reality and writing was such that portions of the second part of this book were written on a lap-top computer while I kept my vigil—first in the hospital, then in the care center—beside the bed where Marian lay unconscious. Portions of Part I were written after she had moved to the nursing facility again. Within a few days after the first draft of the book was finished, Marian died.

With deep appreciation for all that she contributed to this book, and all that she contributed to much more in my life, I dedicate *A Book about Dying* to

Marian Justine Kirven
February 1, 1928–January 19, 1996

∾

Robert H. Kirven
Glendale, Arizona

*A Book
about Dying*

∼

Part I
Goals ～

*T*his book is not about death. It is about living after dying, about how to live before dying so as to prepare for achieving the final goal, and about the transition that we call dying. Thinking about dying as a transition—as the beginning of a new kind of living, as well as the end of our familiar kind of living—may make the death of the body less frightening, less of an enemy, an "end" in only one sense of that word.

When we are young, and at least until we reach that vague plateau called "middle age," it is natural and easy to list goals or ends that we want to reach or accomplish before we die. Later on—perhaps at a milestone birthday that seems to end our middle age—many of us find it difficult to think of our remaining life goals and eventual death at the same time. Juxtaposing those topics raises strong feelings that we try to avoid.

Yet, life goals and our eventual death are converging subjects. Along with the infinite varieties and hierarchies of ends that different individuals pursue, there is one goal—an important one, although intermediate or transitional—that every living person shares and achieves. We call it dying. We set many of our other goals in its shadow, as when we say, "I hope to go here or there, or do this or that, before I die."

But there is another end, an end beyond dying. We were born to live in such a way that we become angels after our physical death. It is for this purpose that we are living now and will die some day. This end can be shared by all, although some people achieve it and become angels, while others choose a different goal and achieve that. However, life among the angels in heaven is a possibility and a hope for everyone.

Those are controversial statements. You might consider them daring. Perhaps you find them foolish. You might be in the minority that considers them obvious. They cannot be proved to you if you want to believe something else. However, there are some indications of their validity, and these indications may assist you if at some level of your consciousness you want to believe them.

What you believe happens after you die makes important differences, both when you approach the time of your death and throughout your dying process itself. Even more important than that, what you believe about living after dying can make a decisive difference in how you live before dying; and that is the most important difference of all.

Human nature is characterized by a desire to live. Many people have supposed that the universal will to live necessarily produces an equal fear of dying. Paul Tillich, perhaps the dominant Protestant theologian of the mid-twentieth century, regarded this fear of dying (including a fear of thus ceasing to *be*) as a determining aspect of human personality. On the other hand, some individuals who have lived to advanced age, or are in semifinal stages of fatal illness, have been regarded with admiration or even awe because they do not display such a fear. Interest in near-death experiences in recent decades has shown that people who apparently know about death from experience seem not to fear facing it for a last time.

It might seem contradictory in theory, but the fact is that the virtually universal desire to live is matched with a far from universal fear of dying. A colleague of mine, in home hospice with cancer in his lungs, feared he might not be able to keep one last preaching commitment or finish all the letters he wanted to write; still, he looked on dying as an end to his pain, an end he had accepted. He did not finish all the letters, but he delivered the sermon beautifully and powerfully. He died soon afterward, as he expected, but not before a deeply moved congregation had shared his conviction that our work in this life is done in a larger context that extends beyond our dying.

Samuel Johnson observed that the prospect of hanging "marvelously focuses the mind," and the same may be said of proximity to death by any means. That focus, aided in some cases by dreams, hallucinations, or more generalized kinds of intuition, has an effect on people who have been seriously ill for some time. That effect is similar to the effect of near-death experiences and their often-spectacular memories: those who know the most about dying usually are the least afraid to do it.

This need not be surprising. Experience or intuition of even the beginning of the dying process shows it to be a transition, rather than an ending. The end of our *body's* life is not the end of *our* life. After death, we continue to live, living in a new way in a new set of circumstances, as the following chapters explain.

I ~

Living in a New Way

ach of us needs many years to sort out and understand the physical life we are living now—if, indeed, we really understand it yet. However, our new
way of living after dying is enough like our old one on
earth that we can build on what we have learned and realize
what we are doing more quickly than we did growing up in
our bodies. Nevertheless, it does take a while, longer for
some than for others, to comprehend our new situation.

Many near-death experiences have included an awareness of the new life's beginning. In most of those, it was
welcoming, beautiful, intensely loving, simultaneously familiar and radically different. Some see their whole life history flashing by like scenes in a videotape played in "fast
forward"; or, in more cases, the scene is described as "spread
out around" them. Some have been taken on "journeys" to
see things that answered questions or problems that had
troubled them deeply. Whatever the details, virtually all reports claim that the person who was near death felt real
and recognizable as herself or himself during the out-of-
body experience. Most accounts also include descriptions
of "a being of light," or other indescribable presences, and
of situations unlike anything ever known in physical life.
By unanimous report, first glimpses of the new way of

living reveal in some respects a seamless continuation of our human life, yet in other ways an existence that is very different.

Further descriptions of the new way of living, more extensive than the brief introduction described by people who only came "near death" before returning to physical life, can be found in reports by Emanuel Swedenborg. Swedenborg was an eighteenth-century scientist who turned to writing theology after he began having almost daily experiences of living beyond physical death. He had the experience of dying-and-waking several times, and was allowed to see others who had died and were awakening from death. He also visited many parts of heaven and hell, as well as the intermediate state that he called "the world of spirits," observing details of how living continues after dying and having conversations with angels. After hundreds of experiences like this, he wrote about spiritual life in the detailed manner of a scientific observer, hoping that his accounts would convince people that the new way of living—spiritual living—is real. Also, he wanted to convince people that it is important to know about that life while we are living in the familiar conditions of physical life. He wrote:

> Of the Lord's Divine mercy it has been granted me now for some years to be constantly and uninterruptedly in company with spirits and angels, hearing them speak and in turn speaking with them. In this way it has been given me to hear and see wonderful things in the other life which have never before come to the knowledge of any one, nor into anyone's idea. I have been instructed in regard to the different kinds of spirits; the state of souls

after death; hell, or the lamentable state of the unfaithful; heaven, or the blessed state of the faithful.

Arcana Coelestia 5[1]

In scattered passages throughout his theological works, and especially in *Heaven and Hell,* his most popular book, Swedenborg recounted his experiences among those who were living beyond their own death, and painted a detailed and consistent picture of their way of living. From those accounts, we can know a lot about spiritual living beyond physical dying.

Really real and really new

After you die, everything about yourself and your life is obviously and unquestionably real. If you pinch yourself, it hurts; but you do not wake up (as from a dream) because you are awake already. If you lean over to smell a flower, you will find your sense of sight, touch, and smell working at least as well as ever, and probably better. In fact, some of the first clues that this plainly real experience is also a new way of living is that your senses are keener. Fragrances are more delightful than any you remember since childhood, the landscape is more beautiful than any you can recall, and the sensation of a light breeze on your face in the sunlight

---

1. All quotations from Emanuel Swedenborg's writings are taken from editions published by the Swedenborg Foundation, West Chester, Pennsylvania, although I have sometimes modernized the English. The number following the volume title refers to a paragraph number. These numbers are uniform in all editions and are used in Swedenborg studies in place of a page number.

awakens a joy in feeling and touching the environment in which you find yourself. People who died with a long-term infirmity recognize the newness right away, for they now walk even if they had been crippled, see their surroundings even if they had been blind, hear the songs of birds and the greetings of old friends even if they had been deaf.

Yes, friends and family members are able to recognize and greet one another, for personal identity continues from physical life into the new way of spiritual living. Loved ones and close friends are real and present in the new way of living as they were before. This is true concerning most of what is really important in physical life. Early awareness of our surroundings and companions so closely resembles the life we have known that many people need a little while to realize that their flesh-and-blood body actually has died. Swedenborg reports:

～

In regard to the general subject of the life of souls—that is, of novitiate spirits—after death, I may state that much experience has shown that when people come into the other life they are not aware that they are in that life, but suppose they are still in this world, and even that they are still in their body. So much is this the case that when they are told that they are a spirit, wonder and amazement possesses them, both because they find themselves exactly like a human being in their senses, desires and thoughts, and because during their life in this world they had not believed in the existence of the spirit—or, as is the case with some, that the spirit could be what they now find it to be.

Arcana Coelestia 320

～

It does not take long, however, to realize that the continuity between the old and the new ways of living is mingled with some radical discontinuity. The restoration of faculties, such as hearing and sight, has already been mentioned; but differences appear as well. Swedenborg listed a few examples that seemed most surprising to him:

⌒

First, communities of spirits and angels appear distinct from one another as to situation, although places and distances in that life are nothing else than varieties of state. Second, situations and distances are determined by their relation to the human [spiritual] body, so that those who are on the right appear on the right whichever way . . . [one turns]; and the case is the same with those who are on the left and in all other directions. Third, no spirits or angels are at so great a distance away that they cannot be seen; and yet no more come into view than so many as the Lord permits. Fourth, spirits of whom others are thinking, for example, such as had been in some manner known to them in the life of the body, are present in a moment (when the Lord permits it), and so closely that they are at the ear, in touch, or else at some distance, greater or less, no matter should they be thousands of miles away, or even among the stars. The reason is that distance of place has no effect in the other life. Fifth, with the angels there is no idea of time. These things are so in the world of spirits, and are still more completely so in heaven. . . .These things seem incredible, but yet they are true.

Arcana Coelestia 1273

⌒

It is easy to get caught up in amazement at what is different and strange about the new kind of living that awaits us, and even to get into fruitless mental debating about whether such things actually could be true. It can be more interesting, and more helpful in the long run, to imagine what it would be like to live in a way in which such things seem natural and what possibilities such new ways of living open for us. Some futuristic science-fiction titillates this natural interest in us, although it often focuses on the strange rather than the helpful aspects of an imaginary way of living. The characteristics of spiritual living not only are real, but all of them turn out to make life better. For this reason they may make spiritual living more understandable and more believable.

Living after dying, you find yourself surrounded by things that reflect your state of mind and in the company of spirits who are very much like you, sharing similar values, interests, and so forth. That may seem natural enough, until you turn your mind to other interests and suddenly find yourself in new surroundings and among other spirits who share these interests or values with you. Even such shifts may not startle you at first, because you are accustomed to things like that happening in your dreams; but at some point it becomes obvious that you can move from one place to another without crossing any intervening space.

This new capability, like others that you gradually become aware of as you need them, turns out to be easy and normal in the spiritual world because the limitations of the physical world no longer apply. You can *be* close to those you love or those who share your interests at the moment under conditions that would allow you only to *feel* close to them in this physical world. After a few trials and errors in the process of judgment when your purely spiritual life begins ("purely" in that it is no longer interdependent with physical reality), you will never find yourself "feeling out of place." Changes in yourself or your environment will happen only when it feels right.

New cartography ~

One characteristic of the new way of living is that distance, dimensions, and other aspects of space in our physical environment do not exist in the spiritual world. Your mental map of your surroundings is composed of new elements. Part of what makes you feel comfortable during your introduction to spiritual living is the fact that things *seem* to have size and dimensions, and things and people *appear* to be close or at a distance. Those appearances arise from the fact that spiritual differences result in separation between things and people, just as distance does in the physical world. That is why we feel that the people who have most in common with us in important respects are "close" to us, and our mental map of our surroundings is based on characteristics and affinities as if they were direction and distance.

Even in this physical life, we can feel close to our spouse or to a friend who works with us for a common cause, even though the two of us are separated by the distance across town or even across the country. In purely spiritual living, that kind of closeness of feelings or of thoughts results in actual proximity. In the new way of living, we will send no spiritual postcards saying "Wish you were here!" We will not send them either because we will find it difficult at first (and impossible before long) to express a thought we do not really mean or because, if we do mean it, the thought would actually bring the person in our mind immediately to our side in the environment we want to share. The physical difficulties which that arrangement would create for popular people living as we do now are not problems in spiritual reality.

Furthermore, the image of vacation that is familiar in physical life—the idea of going someplace you want to be, to be recreated before returning to someplace where you would rather not be—makes little sense (if any at all) in the spiritual world because you live in the place you find most congenial and comfortable out of all the options that exist. If variety is important to you, variety is characteristic of the community in which you live. For the same reason, stability and continuity will be prominent aspects of your home community if that is more important to you. There will be few motivations for getting away from home, and no place where you would rather be.

This makes for a cartography that may be hard to grasp until you have some practice at thinking about distance as a quality of difference rather than an aspect of space. There are groups of dwellings, like small towns, populated by spiritual beings, spirits who share something important with each other but who, as a group, are a minority. There are cities made up of larger groups of people sharing common values, and suburbs of those cities for comparatively similar spirits. There are still larger groupings, too, comparable to states and to nations on our terrestrial globe.

Closeness brought about by similarity, as well as remoteness resulting from difference, produce these kinds of maps. The maps are stable, because of the continuity of spiritual life. The arrangement is not confining, however. Spirits are free to leave one community and join another if and when that is what they really want to do.

New community ∾

Spiritual cartography maps communities of spirits according to their relationship, as spirits within communities relate to one another. Spiritual communities are the primary context of an individual's experience of living beyond death. In a very real sense, a spiritual community is every spirit's link with all of reality and with the source of life. Swedenborg's observation of spirits left him with no doubt about this.

In describing spiritual living, Swedenborg refers to three categories of spiritual beings. He speaks of good spirits, whom he also calls angels, and of bad or evil spirits, whom he sometimes calls devils or satans. Perhaps most frequently he writes of "spirits," a term that he uses sometimes to describe all spiritual beings of any quality, but more often referring to those who have recently left their physical life and have not yet found a home for themselves in either heaven or hell. They live among others like themselves in a special "region" of the spaceless spiritual world that he calls the "world of spirits." He writes:

∾

No angel or spirit can have any life unless he is in some community, and thereby in a harmony of many [spirits]. Indeed no angel, or spirit, or community, can have any life (that is, be affected by anything good, exercise will, be affected by anything true, or even think) unless they are in unity through their community with heaven and with the world of spirits.

Arcana Coelestia 687

∾

It has been fashionable at times in intellectual history (and continues to be among some students beginning philosophy, psychology, or sociology) to analyze human nature by considering the model of an individual alone on a desert island. The exercise has limited value in understanding physical human beings and would have no relation whatever to the way of living that is known in the spiritual world. There, it is plain to everyone who inquires that "no man is an island, entire of itself," as John Donne realized long ago. Living beyond dying is a communal experience. A man truly wanting to be a hermit would find himself in a community of people wanting the same thing—presumably not in heaven, where loving one's neighbors is a universal joy.

Every spirit, angel, and devil receive the power to think, feel, act, even to *be,* by being connected through the societies and communities of the spiritual world to the source of all life—God. That life-giving stream of divine power flows into individuals through the communities in which they live. Angels who truly know themselves recognize their participation in their community and know it in relation to the larger and larger communities and societies and nations of communities in which theirs has its identity.

Individuals relate to one another in their communities in much the same way as cells interact with each other in organs of the physical body; and communities interact with other communities in the way that parts and organs and systems relate to each other in a healthy, living human being. Living the way we do after we die is never lonely. It is a way of living that draws energy, direction, and joy for each individual from his or her common bond with compatible and harmonious spirits.

The community being described is not only a community of spirits that we will join one day after we have died. It also includes us, living now. The core of our being—our spirit, the aspect of our self that lives on after physical death—is related to a spiritual community right now. At the moment these words are written, at the same moment as they are being read, my spirit and yours are connected with a spiritual community. We draw inspiration, guidance, support, life itself, our soul's existence and its ability to maintain our physical body from God. The power to be emanates only from God, but it comes to us only by means of our spiritual companions and communities. Here is Swedenborg's assertion of that remarkable claim:

∾

It is the same with the human race: nobody (regardless of status or position) can live—that is, be affected by anything good, exercise will, be affected by what is true, or even think—unless in like manner they are united with heaven through the angels who are with them; and connected with the world of spirits and, indeed, connected with hell through the spirits that are with them. For every person living in a body is in some society of spirits and of angels, though entirely unaware of it. And if people were not conjoined with heaven and with the world of spirits through the community in which they live, they could not live a moment.

Arcana Coelestia 687

∾

Purely spiritual life is worth knowing about even while we live in physical bodies. What is plainly true in the spiritual world is true for spirits living in earthly bodies as well, although it may not be intuitively obvious in the latter case. We human beings are spirits enveloped in bodies, and both these facets of our human nature are essential to our humanity. Neither aspect is fully human by itself: a bodiless

Part I: Goals

spirit is a ghost, and a spiritless body is a corpse. Spirit and body must interact in harmony if we are to accomplish anything, help anyone, or make any kind of difference by living in the physical world. And the meaning, purpose, and value by which our spirit intends and our body acts unite us with a similarly oriented spiritual community. What we are determines the community that we are related to, and that community helps determine who we are. We are in fellowship with the spiritual world all the time, whether we are conscious of it or not. In fact, we are normally unconscious of our spiritual community and its influences on us, for reasons related to our freedom of choice (as discussed in the next chapter). A special kind of effort is required to reach any consciousness of our spiritual fellowship while we live in the physical world. In the new life that we will be living after our body dies, our sense of community becomes much more prominent in our thoughts.

18 ~

2 ~

Continuing Identity

ontinuing personal identity is an essential characteristic of our life after we die. It controls our spiritual
self-realization, our fellowship, and home community; and it explains the supreme importance that is entailed
by the choices we make during our physical life. In his visits
to the spiritual world, Emanuel Swedenborg met neophyte
spirits who were surprised to find themselves alive—so
solid, not at all vaporous or gauzy—in such a tangible environment. On the other hand, he never met any spirits who
wondered who they were, or doubted in the slightest degree that they were the same person they had been while
living in their physical body.

Wherever you go, there you are ~

This is a phrase heard frequently in a variety of self-help and
twelve-step groups. People often tell of failed attempts to
solve old problems by means of "geographical cures"—that
is, moving to a new location to "start over again." Unless
they are accompanied by other strongly supporting elements,
attempts of this kind usually have foundered on the dilemma
that is summarized, "Wherever you go, there you are." Since
the fundamental cause of most successes or failures lies

within us rather than in people, places, and things around us, a change of scene only provides a new backdrop for acting out our familiar habits and compulsions. Since each human spirit already is connected with a spiritual community, it may not be surprising that we will come into full consciousness in that community with the same values, hopes, and intentions that we held before physical death. If our inner and outer interests, preferences, and intentions are the same, we may awake after dying in the community that will be our home. More likely, we will arrive in the spiritual world in a community of neophyte spirits who, like us, still have a lot of sorting-out and self-discovery to do to find their true home; and even that may be a place to move from again as we continue to grow and develop.

In fact, the transition from physical-and-spiritual to purely spiritual makes continuity of identity even more significant than it is in so-called geographical cures. If you move from Minneapolis to San Diego, you will find yourself dealing with the same inner problems in the sunshine as you did in the snow; but in both locations you have equal opportunities to change yourself. The transition from this earthly life to the new spiritual one is more radical, however.

So long as you are a spirit enveloped in a physical body, your two qualities—spirit and flesh—form a dynamically balanced tension with each other. That tension tends to force decisions and makes change of your whole nature easier than it could be under any other conditions. Your body wants comfort, satisfaction, and control over its surroundings and neighbors (and needs these things, to some extent). Your spirit is influenced by these physical desires, as well as by spiritual influences, some of which draw you toward love and concern for others, delight in a neighbor's success, and the kinds of goals we call altruistic. These counteracting influences press us toward choices that align us more closely with one facet or another of our lives, and these choices shape the character that stays with us in the new way of living.

After we die, the absence of one pole of that built-in tension between body and spirit leaves us in a different situation regarding life choices and character-building. Our nature in that new environment remains able to learn, grow, and change; but our motivation for change is so different that major transformations become more difficult and less likely.

This means that most spirits enter their new way of living with values and preferences that eventually will unite them with the community where they will feel eternally at home. We will see how it takes some spirits longer than others to recognize what their most fundamental values and preferences are, but few change them (or the community where they feel at home) after that realization.

There are many things in this physical life that we cannot control, but one that we can (perhaps, in some cases, the *only* thing we can control) is this: we are forever free to choose what we want to want. That may not seem like much if you live in relatively free and fortunate circumstances; but that particular formulation of the irreducible human freedom of choice owes much to psychologist Victor Frankl, who discovered in a Nazi death camp that just that freedom alone was motive enough to live. That irreducible freedom also includes our ability to choose the values that will determine the community in which we will find our eternal home. It is a choice based less on what we have been able to do (though the critical importance of our actions will be seen later) than what we want to do at the deepest and most interior levels of our mind and being.

That heartfelt want, that inmost desire, may not be evident to anyone around us in the material world. As a matter of fact, many of us hide it from our own self-consciousness. But at some level, that core intention—Swedenborg calls it our "life's love"—is there to be recognized when we are ready. It already is known to God. As the psalmist wrote: "If I ascend to heaven, Thou art there; If I make my bed in Hell, behold, Thou art there!" As they say, with the wisdom of experience, wherever you go, there you are!

Meeting old friends ～

For many spirits awaking from death, the first realization that they are living in a new way comes when they greet friends or loved ones whom they know to have died before them. I know of one woman who happily greeted her dead spouse a few moments before she died; and many carefully documented case studies in the files of the British and American societies for psychical research offer many similar accounts. Swedenborg saw it happen to spirits with much greater frequency soon after their deaths. Knowing what we do about the continuity of identity and the natural harmony of spiritual community, it is not surprising that people with whom we had close emotional bonds during physical life would be in the community, or at least the neighborhood, in which we will find our first spiritual consciousness. It also is not surprising that being there, they would be among the first to greet us.

Meetings of this kind have multiple values for neophytes in the new way of living. For one thing, as just mentioned, it offers a gentle clue, if they need one, that they are now in the realm where people live after dying. For another, it provides the comfort of a familiar and trusted companion in what some spirits (but certainly not all) find to be a difficult transition. Still another benefit is the increased confidence that comes from being introduced to what feels like a new community by an old friend instead of a stranger—however perceptive and loving that stranger may be.

This confidence, however reassuring to the newly awakened spirit, is based on an illusion of privacy. After a period of acclimation, each spirit realizes that the nature of spiritual life includes a kind of transparency that makes a spirit's characteristic values and intentions obvious to everyone who meets him or her. The ability to dissemble—to smile politely when meeting a personal opponent, to assume an air of supreme confidence to cover a feeling of uncertainty—is used so commonly in physical life that it often is assumed to be a normal convention. That ability to dissemble is so powerful, in fact, that we can succeed at hiding our true intentions and values from ourselves. In the spiritual world, a few spirits retain that ability (or seem to themselves to retain it) for a little while, but inevitably it falls away. Angels become angels, and devils become devils, by knowing who they are and what they most prize and desire; and all their companions know it, too. The apparent stranger who introduces those who have recently died to their home community actually knows the neophytes as well (and probably much better) than they know themselves.

The radical honesty that spiritual nature imposes on that new way of living also explains why some friends who had been very close in physical life greet each other with joy but gradually begin to drift apart. In such cases, the friendship had been based more on appearances than essential compatibility, and loses its bonding power in the spiritual world. Swedenborg explains:

～

In the other life those meet together, when they so desire, who have been in some conjunction in the world, either by love, or by friendship, or by high regard; but they are afterward separated according to the unlikenesses of their state of life.

Arcana Coelestia 9104

～

The same aspect of life also assures that friendships formed in purely spiritual life will be enduring and mutually satisfying. Transparent intentions lead to more gratifying associations, and fewer unpleasant surprises, than the poker-faced conventions of physical life.

Rejoining spouses ～

For many people, the bond with a spouse is the most significant relationship of their entire physical life, involving the greatest range of physical, emotional, and spiritual experiences of union. These are the people who would declare, as Elizabeth Barrett Browning put it, "I love you with the breath, smiles, tears, of all my life; and, if God choose, I shall but love you better after death."

Those fortunate enough to enjoy a marriage that inspires this kind of hope will find strong assurances from Swedenborg's observations of the way of living that transcends death. A man and a woman who have grown together into the kind of relationship he calls "truly marital" are promised that their union like their love will be eternal. In fact, most married couples can expect to continue their marriage as they continue living; and if one dies before the other, the bond between them will remain during the interim before they meet again in purely spiritual living. If the physically surviving spouse is open to such feelings and intuitions, the bond at times may be a conscious one for both of them. People who marry more than once in this life can have a mutually supporting and satisfying relationship in both (or more) marriages, without forming a "truly marital" bond with more than one spouse.

On the other hand, people who feel trapped in a marriage that is maintained for a reason other than mutual love between the husband and wife need not fear being trapped in that relationship eternally. All angels in heaven live as married couples, but only as couples enjoying truly marital love. People who are unmarried in physical life, or married in a relationship that is not truly marital, find a partner with whom such mutual love is possible after they begin living in the purely spiritual way. The transparent honesty of spirits about matters that are most important to the development of truly marital love and the natural tendency of harmonious spirits to be close to one another make this mate-finding easier than we could imagine on the basis of physical experience alone.

Emanuel Swedenborg, for example, had sought marriage with two different women, both of whom married someone else; but in his physical old age, he was allowed to learn during his visits in the spiritual realm who his partner in eternal marriage love would be. She was a woman he had known in Stockholm, first as the wife of a friend of his and later as a widow. Her former husband having found his true marital mate in the world of spirits before she died, she began her purely spiritual life waiting (for an interval outside of time) for Swedenborg to join her eternally after his physical death.

While such knowledge of spiritual relationships is not as

accessible to most of us as it was to Swedenborg during the period of his daily spiritual experiences, the arrangement is universal for all who have built for themselves, by the choices made during their physical lifetime, a capacity for mutual love with a person of the opposite sex. Swedenborg speaks briefly and negatively about same-sex sexual relationships. He apparently had no acquaintance with spirits who had felt their spiritual gender to be mismatched with their physical body, so he said little that applies unequivocally to modern issues of homosexual relationships.

In any event, the capacity for mutual love with another person is characteristic of those who find their home in a heavenly community, and a spouse will be found there for those who arrive without a marital relationship already established. People who are not capable of mutual love could not feel at home in heaven and would not want to live in that community.

There is more to be said about living in marriage after dying. Swedenborg devoted a whole book to the subject, *Delitiae Sapientiae de Amore Conjugiali.* It has been translated into English under a variety of titles, including *Marriage Love, Marital Love, Conjugial Love,* and, in the most recent translations, *Love in Marriage* and *Married Love.*

3 ∾
New "Space," New "Time"

*A*ttempts to define reality as we perceive it with our physical senses focus to a large extent on elements of space, time, and direction. Our sense of identity, our feeling of being distinguishable from other people, has a lot to do with the spaces we occupy and the space between us and other people and things. Our experience of living depends on time—the amount of time things take to happen, the time at which they happen, the time between events, and whether they are on time. Also, physical time and space are interrelated. We speak of "a space of time" or a "short" or "long" time, and we often indicate the distance between home and work by the time it takes us to get from one place to the other.

Spirits and angels experience something like time and space in the spiritual world, but understand them quite differently than we do on earth. What looks to spirits like dimensions in space really are qualities of spiritual state or condition, and what feels like the passing of time actually is progression through the process of change. Spiritual distance and change are interrelated in much the same was as distance and elapsed time. Swedenborg tells of one experience that offers an extreme example:

❦

Remoteness in the other life does not arise from distance of place; but from difference of state, which nevertheless appears there like distance of place. That is why the two days it took to get [to a certain planet in a psychic experience] enabled me to infer that the state of the interiors with those people—which is the state of the affections and the consequent thoughts—differed in the same proportion from the state of the interiors with the spirits from our earth.

Arcana Coelestia 9967

❦

In other words, those spirits were so different (so distant, spiritually) that it took him two days of continuous and progressive changing to become different enough to be able to visit them! Similarly, accounts of near-death experiences often describe the sensation of travelling very fast ("faster than a jet plane" in one woman's childhood experience) before the person sees things from a point of view he or she had not had before.

Difference and distance ❦

Appearances of space in spiritual living reveal specific details about the quality of things or spirits we may see in that way of living. While the distance at which a thing is seen indicates its difference from us, its length shows us how good a thing it is, its width lets us know how true it is, and its height suggests its spiritual value. In spiritual and in physical vision, shorter distances give us clearer views of the dimensions or qualities of whatever we are looking at. Such differ-

ences of range can be very significant because spiritual vision is so acute that when God allows it—protecting us in
other ways from the overwhelming confusion it could
cause—we can see everything, no matter how remote or
different from us.

Within the range of ordinary concern (and consequent
visual capability), angels and spirits recognize intuitively
how different others are from their own spiritual state and
simultaneously realize the specific ways in which others are
different—more or less good, more or less true. The importance of knowing these things lies partly in the consideration that living after dying is a dynamic experience of
development and progress, punctuated by periods of rest
and consolidation. This aspect of spiritual reality is reflected
in biblical stories of the Israelites travelling for years and
decades with their nomad-style tents, as Swedenborg explained in *Arcana Coelestia* 1293. These stories picture "living" as "dwelling in tents"—tents that can be taken down
each morning and set up the next night through the course
of a journey. Being able to look ahead, to know how much
change (and what kind of change) will be necessary to
reach a goal, is helpful to spirits in their life—that is, on
their journey.

Just as pioneers crossing the American continent in
wagon trains knew how high or how wide and how far off
were the mountains and rivers they would have to cross, because they sent scouts to look ahead, so the kinds of environmental information that spirits need are available to
them through what looks like distance and dimension.
Seeing differences, and qualities of differences, seems as natural in that way of living as seeing distances and dimensions
does in physical life.

Time for change ∼

Carefully analyzing what we know of time—at least, that time that we measure by clocks, by the sun or the stars, or even by carbon dating—may make plain why time does not continue in the new way of living that we know after dying. Clocks, our sun and stars, and carbon-14 isotopes, all are part of the physical environment that we leave behind when we begin that life. The spiritual realities that the sun and stars and their rhythmic cycles represent do exist in the spiritual environment, but they have nothing to do with minutes and hours, or days, weeks, months, or years.

Of course, there is another meaning that we sometimes intend when we speak of time. We say, "It's about time," when something happens after we have been waiting for it; "It's time I started supper," often referring more to a feeling of hunger than to the time on the clock. Mark's gospel quotes Jesus as saying, "The time is fulfilled, and the kingdom of God is at hand" (1:15). None of these uses of "time" refers to clocks or calendars, but rather to a sense of appropriateness, or readiness, or completion of preparations. Greek, the original language of the New Testament and of early philosophers who played a major role in forming the patterns of Western thinking, avoids that confusion by using two separate words for those two meanings of "time." One is *chronos*, from which we get chronometers and chronology; and the other is *kairos*—the word that Matthew attributed to Jesus, speaking of a time that was *éggiken*, "at hand," a time that could be *peplérotai*, "fulfilled."

The *kairos* kind of time is determined, even in our physical experience, by spiritual conditions and values, so it might be expected to be part of our spiritual thinking. Theologians speak of a "kairos moment," as the point at which spiritual values break into human affairs. The *chronos* kind of time, however, is an artifact of our measuring and keeping count of physical properties. It does not follow us into the new life.

There is, as well, a third meaning for time. It has no separate Greek word to distinguish it, but it feels like *chronos*, although it is more related to *kairos*. This is the meaning we intend when we talk of how "time dragged so slowly," or "I was so fascinated that the hour just seemed to *fly* by." Our personal sensation of the passing of time may become fairly well coordinated with the passing of clock time if we compare them often, or have years of practice at some job where events are carefully ordered. But children—and most of us, especially in relaxed moments or in periods of unusual stress—feel time going by in a highly subjective way that is determined mostly by whether we enjoy or dislike what is happening or expected to happen. Swedenborg referred to this common usage to illustrate the partial awareness of spiritual reality that can come to us in ordinary experience.

༚

> Some [people] know that times [derive from] states, for they know that times are in exact accord with the states of their affections, short to those who are in pleasant and joyous states, long to those who are in unpleasant and sorrowful states, and various in a state of hope and expectation.
>
> *Heaven and Hell* 168(3)

༚

In purely spiritual living, the intuition behind this linguistic convention is tangible fact. Spirits and angels all pass through progressive series of states just as we progress through morning, noon, and evening, or spring, summer, and fall; but they have no fixed intervals by which these states are experienced. Angels and spirits remember the states that they have experienced, recalling some more clearly and easily than others, just as we remember the days and seasons and years of our physical life. Both kinds of experience are similar, but no spiritual experience ever is cut short because a bell rang, or the sun went down, or the clock struck: each experience, unshackled from the rigidity of our time, runs its full course according to its inner, spiritual dynamics.

New directions ~

Just as time is measured most easily in our physical world by the earth's rotation (what looks from our vantage point as the revolution of the sun around the earth), so directions can be recognized by our relation to the sun. It seems to rise in the east, progress upward and to the south (in the northern hemisphere), and set in the west. Swedenborg describes the first appearance of the spiritual environment as being very similar, and the next level of awareness as very different.

~

> In heaven, where the Lord is seen . . . is called the east. Opposite to this is west, at the right is south. . . and at the left the north. This [continues to be true, no matter] in whatever direction the face and body are turned.
>
> *Heaven and Hell* 141

~

Angels always face toward God, no matter which way they turn their bodies, which Swedenborg ranks in *Heaven*

and Hell 144 as "one of heaven's wonders," including the phe-
nomenon of a group of angels facing in different directions
while the sun is in front of each of them at the same time,
and the angels' mental capability of looking to the south,
west, or north without turning their body or their head!

Swedenborg realized that such a wonder is hard to imagine on the basis of our experience with physical directions,
but he found no better way of describing it. The situation
may be comprehended somewhat more fully if the nature of
the spiritual world's sun is more thoroughly explained. That
explanation, however, requires a short detour to define one
of Swedenborg's most important terms, "The Lord."

At the beginning of his theological work *Arcana Coelestia*
(§14), Swedenborg explains that "in the following pages . . .
by the Lord is meant Jesus Christ." In a later treatise, *True
Christian Religion* (§26), he expanded his terminology to
greater precision: "God is Jesus Christ, who is the Lord . . .
Creator from eternity, Redeemer in time, and Regenerator
to eternity. Thus the Lord is at once Father, Son, and Holy
Spirit." He points to the long Hebraic tradition of reading
Adonai, or "Lord," for the divine name YHWH; and Jesus'
instruction to his disciples to call him "Lord" (John 13:13).

In the preceding quotation, therefore, "the Lord" appearing as the sun in heaven's sky is to be understood as the
risen Christ, embodying the entire triune God. Angels
know that the sun in their sky is the Lord, but they see a
sun: even the highest angels cannot look directly at the full
glory of God. But that sun, the Lord, is the focus of all life,
love, and intention: all angels face that sun always and determine all relationships in accordance with it.

Something similar happens with all spirits throughout
the spiritual world, but spirits outside of heaven are not all
directed toward the Lord.

4 ～
Coming Home

*T*he beginning of each spirit's new way of living after the body dies is a somewhat protracted process of finding a home in one of the seemingly infinite variety of communities in the societies and nations of societies that make up the spiritual world. Some of these communities are heavenly, and taken together are called heaven; some are hellish and as a group are called hell; and some are between heaven and hell, in what is called the world of spirits, and are temporary homes for neophyte spirits who have not yet found the home best suited to them. There are as many kinds of communities as there are kinds of people in the world. As has been noted already, each person living in a physical body is connected to a spiritual community that harmonizes with the values and intentions that guide his or her life.

Living in this physical world, people become skilled at giving the appearance of having spiritual goals that are different from the ones they follow most consistently (even follow subconsciously). They appear to their friends in their physical community to be quite different from their actual spiritual character. Sometimes, they even convince themselves that they really are the kind of person they appear to be. That is possible because many attitudes and activities can have a good effect and make the person doing them look good, even when the person's motives are self-serving or evil in other ways. Therefore, people do not always know the kind of spiritual community with which they are associated. That is most obviously true for people who do not think about or believe in the existence of any kind of spiritual community.

To find their home community and their place in it, people have first to come to a recognition of their deepest, truest, spiritual character—the way they have *chosen* to live, regardless of claims and appearances. Then, they must find a community where a soul of that nature can feel at home. This search for home begins after the first awakening and realization of the new way of living. Swedenborg described this way of coming home:

∾

Souls newly arrived from the world, when about to leave the company of the spiritual angels [who first welcomed them to the new way of living], go among spirits, and so at length come into the society in which they had been while they lived in the body, are led about by angels to many mansions or abodes, that is, to societies that are distinct and yet conjoined with others; in some of which they are received, while in other cases they are led to still other societies. This [process continues] for an indefinite time, until they come to the society in which they had been while they lived in the body; and there they remain. . . . I have been led through such "mansions" in like manner, and those who dwelt there conversed with me, so that I might know how [this was].

Arcana Coelestia 1273

∾

Coming Home, Belonging, Feeling Comfortable

All spirits eventually find the hellish or heavenly community with which they had customarily associated during their physical life. <u>There they feel truly "at home" and comfortable</u> especially by comparison with every other place they had visited before, thinking that place or that group would be <u>a congenial home.</u> <u>That feeling of belonging,</u> made more vivid by the recent experiences of not belonging, indicates to the spirits that they have come home at last.

Time for judgment ～

For many Christians, there is one startling surprise in Swedenborg's reports of his observations of the kind of living that follows dying. Although there is a hell as well as a heaven in that realm, there is no judge or court to sentence spirits to hell or send them to heaven. There is no "last trumpet," no opening of the "Book of Life," no pleading at the "Throne of God." All these symbols, no longer necessary for human understanding, refer to the process of self-discovery, just described, by which <u>spirits choose their own home in heaven or in hell.</u> This is the process set forth for the popular imagination, in an era when everyone was ruled by despots, of a "Last Judgment." The decision is a pragmatic one, in a way, as spirits "try out" different communities as young people in physical life sometimes experiment with different "life styles," until they <u>realize what feels right and natural for them.</u> But its basis in experience makes the self-judgment more compelling than the decision of any judge with any number of jailers to enforce the judgments. <u>Each</u> <u>spirit chooses a home that feels right because, in the whole spiritual universe of possibilities, it is the one perfect fit for</u>

Our spiritual/nature is shaped by our own choices.

Part I: Goals *Value: What we love most dearly and most deeply want to do (Intend)*

> the particular character of intentions and values that the individual forged by the whole pattern of decisions in the course of physical living.
>
> That character is formed far less by what we actually accomplish than (by what we value and intend)—what we love most dearly and most deeply want to do. That is why our spiritual nature is shaped by our own choices, rather than by the opportunities life has presented to us. The English poet

Thomas Gray observed in "Elegy Written in a Country Churchyard" that "some mute inglorious Milton" might be resting unknown, beside "some Cromwell, guiltless of his country's blood." The continuing life of those two spirits would be characterized by the undiscovered Milton's sensitive creativity and by the physically guiltless Cromwell's inner cruelty.

Swedenborg takes care to explain that this is the kind of judgment described in the Bible (in passages where the literal sense has made some people imagine a judge on a throne, passing sentences, and hell as a lake of fire):

∿

It is frequently said in the [Bible] that people will be judged and will be rewarded according to their deeds and works, referring to internal origins of "deeds and works" (not in their external form, since good works in external form are likewise done by wicked people, but in their internal and external form together good works are done only by good people.) Works, like all activities, have their being and result and quality from the interiors of the thought and will of the person doing them.

Heaven and Hell 358 (note 1)

∿

→ a person is a person by virtue of his ability to intend what is good and loving and to discern what is true and wise.

In other words, what you believe to be good and right and what you really hope to accomplish by what you are trying to do are the criteria that determine the kind of person you are. What you actually do and what may result from it can be influenced by many factors outside your control. But the values and intentions behind your actions, the hidden goals and motives that drive what you do, are the products of your lifetime of decisions up to now, and a force that shapes your nature that will guide your future actions. No judge needs to declare your character "good" or "wicked" because your own judgments throughout your physical lifetime have made you one or the other. In living after dying, the result of that character-building is plain for all to see.

The judgment that really determines our nature and our home for eternal living is not one that awaits us after death: it is the judgment by which we make our day-to-day choices in the physical life we are living now. The cumulative result of those decisions or judgments shapes our character and determines the spiritual companionship we have now, and that companionship helps to reenforce the direction and pattern of our decisions.

The direction and pattern of living decisions not only *belong* to us: They are what we have come to be. The choices that have become habitual are who we are.

Finding yourself ∽

The first step spirits must take toward finding their home is finding themselves. The kind of deceit by which we can fool ourselves while our spirit lives in a body already has been suggested and is exposed in purely spiritual living.

There are various ways this can happen. Swedenborg describes schools, taught by angels who love to teach and are very good at it, where spirits entering the new way of living can learn what is true about things they had misunderstood while they were living their physical life.

There is nothing compulsory about these classes, except the spirits' inner compulsion to learn. The teaching angels make no attempt to change their students' attitudes, values, or goals—those aspects of their character that were formed by their choices in physical living—but only to correct their understanding of spiritual realities. People who loved to follow the teachings of their religion take that love with them into heaven; but if they had been taught the teachings of a god who does not actually exist, they have the opportunity in these schools to learn about the Lord, who really rules heaven and earth. When they come to know the Lord as creator, redeemer, and regenerator of all living, the love that they had felt for the highest good they knew turns easily to the highest good there is.

Besides the schools, there are other forms of more individual instruction. People with a real desire to know something, however specialized or esoteric, find that they attract angels who are particularly informed about that particular subject and enjoy nothing more than sharing their knowledge. Swedenborg met angels like this who helped him learn what he needed to know in order to teach people about such things as continuing life. Sometimes an angel would discuss a topic with him. Other times, an angel would take him to hear spirits debate various sides of a subject. Such experiences deepened his understanding, but the angels always made clear that the most important truths he learned did not come even from their great wisdom, but (as he said several times) they came from the Lord alone.

The majority of spirits trying to find themselves as they learn to live after dying do so by the kind of experience already described: they go from place to place (that is, from one spiritual community to another), visiting the places that look attractive, talking with spirits whose goals and values seem similar to ones they had claimed to hold or believed themselves to follow. If their deepest, truest "life's love" is actually harmonious with the community they visit, they stay there. If not, they keep looking.

Preferences and purposes that have been deeply held in physical life but also deeply repressed may be hard to admit as one's own, even in the light of the world of spirits. Some spirits, continuing to deny their own true motives, try so hard to stay in communities where they want to think they are compatible, even though they are not, that they have literally to be forced to leave. Swedenborg saw a few who had to be punished before they realized the actual incompatibility, as he described in *Arcana Coelestia* 1273. Most spirits, however, recognize the harmony or discord for themselves. When there is a big gap between their professed intentions and their real ones, they visit the kind of community they think they would harmonize with, but soon find themselves as desperately uncomfortable there as a fish out of water. Their departure is not only voluntary, but impetuous and hurried.

The home that every spirit eventually comes to is one he or she recognizes, and in which the spirit feels a sense of fitting and belonging. It is a custom-made niche that each of us shapes and confirms for ourselves as the one place in the one community that we claim for our own.

Finding yourself at home ∾

Most people try to make their physical home a reflection of themselves. Some people try harder than others; and of those who try, some have greater success than others. People with a "gift," an "eye," a "touch," for decorating will select color schemes, furnishings, art, and other elements that they "like"—that means that the whole collection of things, when assembled, presents an environment that reflects the decorator's mood or spiritual state. Sometimes, a skilled decorator who is aware of specific effects projected by certain elements creates a room or a home that is a reflection of the spiritual condition he or she would like to have or would wish to become accustomed to. Others, much less concerned with appearances, create a vivid portrait of their inner state precisely by not taking time or trouble to arrange things the way they think things ought to be. A writer's cluttered study, strewn with a variety of papers and objects having no obvious connection, might be a good example, illustrating the chaotic mental state out of which (it is hoped) ideas come together as words in sentences and paragraphs.

Because these environments are physical, however, it always is possible—and it usually is easy—to project an ephemeral or partially false impression. A homemaker might make a home present one image to guests and another to family. The office of a "middle manager" might reflect quite a different personality and character when a superior pays an expected visit than it does when a co-worker comes in on a busy afternoon.

That our surroundings tend to mirror our inner state because we arrange for them to do so is characteristic of physical life as we have always known it. That our sur-

We are what we are, The law of Spiritual Attraction:
We attract to ourselves what we are.

Coming Home

roundings reflect our spiritual condition, despite any efforts of ours to create a different impression, is a minor and undependable aspect of physical life, but it typifies the norm in spiritual living. In the spiritual world, the landscaping and exterior appearance of our home are infallible representations of our spiritual condition. Each room of our home after dying reflects one or another aspect of our life's love and our different roles in life.

We do not have to decorate our home when we find it, for our life in the physical world has built the house and decorated the rooms already. When we find our home after we have died, we recognize it immediately. When we enter it, we know instinctively which drawer in which room contains our socks, our writing paper, or whatever else we might need in beginning our new way of living.

When we find ourselves, we are near our home. When we find our home, we feel completely "at home" in it immediately. The place (or state) in which we feel at home might come as a surprise if we could see it clearly while still living in our physical body. If we have delusions of grandeur, we might expect a fine palace for our heavenly home, but actually find ourselves comfortable only in an unimpressive cottage. If some unconscious need has led us to cultivate an unrealistically poor self-image, we might well be surprised by the large size and opulent furnishings of our spiritual home. In living as we have known it so far, "things are seldom what they seem," to borrow from Gilbert and Sullivan's *H.M.S. Pinafore*. In living after dying, things are never anything else.

That is good news about the new way of living, even if our physical experience suggests it might be threatening. Because we are what we really are, without pretension, and because our surroundings reflect our true spiritual condition, we find ourselves completely at home there. If we find ourselves at home in some region of hell, it is because we cannot be ourselves and be comfortable anywhere else; and we are not uncomfortable or "out of place" in the home we have built for ourself. The "punishment" in hell usually can be described in the words of of Sartre's play *No Exit*. Just before the final curtain descends, a character says, "*L'enfer, c'est l'autres*" (hell is the others). For a thief to live among thieves, for example, always trying to protect things from the thief next door and forever seeking to steal from an equally clever thief may be "a hell of a life," but it is a way of living in which the thief is experienced and well prepared—one that he has chosen and embraced.

For a poor couple, who lived in shabby homes because they could not afford better while raising a family and helping their friends and working hard in their neighborhood, to awake after dying and find themselves in a spacious and comfortable home might raise a momentary question in their minds as to whether someone had made a mistake. But the mistake would be theirs, for thinking their external poverty actually characterized them, rather than their inner wealth. It would take very little experience of living there and meeting their neighbors so much like themselves for them to recognize their spiritual home as truly their own— a reflection of the open, caring, loving (and lovely!) values and intentions that had characterized their living in the physical world.

Our spiritual home feels like home to us because it is the home we have built with the decisions and the actions of our lives. It feels like home because it reflects our life's loves so faithfully that no one else could live there, and we could not live anywhere else!

Excerpted from: *A Book about Dying*
(*Preparing for Eternal Life*)
by *Robert H. Kirven* (1997)

5 ~
Evidence in regard to Emanuel Swedenborg's Credibility

*T*his book has made some startling claims: people continue living after they die, and living after dying happens in the way it has been described here. The primary witness in support of these claims, whose detailed reports underlie almost all that has been said, is Emanuel Swedenborg. This is not the place for a full account of the man's life; but it seems appropriate to say enough about Swedenborg to suggest his credibility as a witness and to summarize some of the explanations that he offered as reasons that his accounts might be believed. It can be pointed out as well, that many people who have read extensively in the theological works that he published between 1748 and 1771 have found internal coherence and consistency in their detailed reports and cogent reasoning that strongly support trust in his reports. To keep all the cards on the table, let me state clearly that this author is among them.

Emanuel Swedenborg ~

What makes a reliable observer and reporter? A reputation for personal integrity and for honesty in reports that can be checked are important qualities. Swedenborg was respected by members of the Swedish parliament, by members of the court of all the monarchs who ruled Sweden during his adult life—and by those monarchs themselves—as a man of learning, probity, and practical knowledge, as well as good company at dinners and other social events. Another quality that would help to qualify an observer would be training and experience in careful observation and detailed reporting. In this connection, it can be noted that Swedenborg was a graduate of Uppsala University, Sweden's premier center of learning at the time. He traveled several times to England and continental Europe to study sciences and technologies that were not available in Sweden. He published his country's first scientific journal *Northern Daedalus*; and in 1734 published a three-volume work on mineralogy that was widely regarded in Europe as defining the state of knowledge of mining and smelting for his time. He had published extensively in physiology as well.

To these credentials as a public figure, a scientific observer and writer, Swedenborg himself once added some further qualifications in a letter to his English friend the Rev. Thomas Hartley, who had asked for some biographical information. Swedenborg wrote to Hartley that he was a fellow of the Swedish Royal Academy of Sciences and that his distinguished family included three bishops, an archbishop, and a provincial governor. He then added, "But all [this] I consider of comparatively little importance; for it is far exceeded by the circumstance that I have been called to a holy office by the Lord himself."[2]

---

2. The full text of Swedenborg's letter to Hartley can be found in Emanuel Swedenborg, *Posthumous Theological Works*, vol. 1 (West Chester, Penn.: The Swedenborg Foundation, 1996), 1–4. It can also be found in R. L. Tafel, ed., *Documents concerning the Life and Character of Emanuel Swedenborg*, vol. 1, doc. 2 (London: Swedenborg Society, 1875), 6–9.

That last qualification, which meant so much to Swedenborg, is perhaps the most dubious credential to a skeptic. While reputation and scientific accomplishment might recommend him as a reporter, a claim to divine commission raises a whole new set of questions. While those questions must be respected, the fact remains that no amount of credibility as a reporter would have gained for Swedenborg the prolonged and unrestricted access to the realm of spirit and continuing life that was provided to enable him to carry out his mission as a writer and a teacher.

These two claims—one, that Swedenborg was divinely commissioned and specially enabled; and two, that he had virtually unlimited access to heaven, hell, and the world of spirits—stand together in a special interrelationship. Either might be difficult to accept alone, but the two together provide mutually explanatory support. The validity of the divine commission is supported by the detailed consistency of what Swedenborg wrote in fulfilling it, and the possibility of his spiritual experiences can be explained by the power of God to enable what is commissioned.

Swedenborg recognized the difficulty some readers might have in accepting these claims and offered a defense. At the end of the first chapter of *Arcana Coelestia* (§68), his first and largest theological work (eight volumes in Latin, twelve volumes in English), he wrote:

∾

I am well aware that many will say that no one can possibly speak with spirits and angels so long as he lives in the body; and many will say that it is all fancy, others that I tell such stories in order to gain credence, and others will make other objections. But by all this <u>I am not deterred,</u> for *I have seen, I have heard, I have felt.*[3]

His expectations of what many would say were realistic enough, but what of his response? <u>It carries the ring of certainty common to a number of eyewitnesses to events so unusual that such witnesses expect to be doubted:</u> "I saw it with my own eyes." Such a defense cannot be established beyond doubt, of course, but neither can any argument dissuade the witness. In Swedenborg's case, the absolute <u>certainty bestowed by the evidence of sight, hearing, and touch left no doubt in his own mind.</u> Yet he realized that fulfilling his commission would require convincing readers of the truth of what he wrote.

Swedenborg apparently realized that an objection might be raised to his reports or his claimed commission. Someone might object that what Swedenborg saw, heard, and felt may have seemed real enough to him; but it might also be special esoteric knowledge and therefore not relevant to common human experience. <u>The answer to that objection, Swedenborg decided, would be an explanation of the full range of human potential.</u>

Human beings were created by the Lord in such a way as to be able to speak with spirits and <u>angels</u> while living in the body, <u>as in fact was done in the most ancient times;</u> for, being spirits clothed with bodies, they are one with them. But because in process of time people so immersed themselves in corporeal and worldly things as to care al-

---

3. The italics are mine, not Swedenborg's.

most nothing for anything else, the way was closed. Yet as soon as the corporeal things recede in which people are immersed, <u>the way is again opened</u>, and they are among spirits, and in a common life with them.

Arcana Coelestia 69

◌

By this explanation, what was made possible for Swedenborg was simply a restoration of abilities that were innate to human nature, but lost in the process of development that led to civilization and human domination of the natural environment. According to this theory, the possibility of experiences like Swedenborg's might be independently confirmed by similar experiences of at least a few people who live somewhat loosely with "corporeal and worldly" things.

Natural human depths ◌

As a matter of fact, such experiences are more common than is generally supposed. In addition to near-death experiences, which reveal a reality not at all unlike the spiritual world that Swedenborg describes, <u>hypnogogic experiences (things that happen while partly awake but also partly asleep)</u> are shared by far more people and also have supporting similarities to Swedenborg's accounts.

<u>Two psychologists</u> who have related extensive clinical experience to their own meditative experiences are <u>Ira Progoff</u> and Wilson Van Dusen. Progoff's *Depth Psychology and Modern Man* (1959) and Van Dusen's *The Natural Depth in Man* (1972) <u>present extensive scientific evidence that under certain conditions people are able to become aware of a real aspect of their life quite apart from physical living.</u>

49 ◌

Evidence of such a reality supports Swedenborg's con-
tention that he saw, heard, and felt things in a realm of reality outside our familiar one.

My own life includes a number of episodes of a similar
kind, which are recounted in *Angels in Action* (1994); and
friends have told me of experiences of theirs that provide
more supporting testimony of the same kind. The common
basis for the events described by Progoff, Van Dusen, and a
number of others is the fundamental human capability to be
affected by the spiritual realm. When deliberate intent (as in
prayer or meditation) or particular psychic need withdraws
our consciousness sufficiently out of the physical sensations
and worldly concerns of our normal preoccupation, we become aware of spiritual influences or the presence of spirits
themselves. Recollection and consideration of this kind of
events have induced in many people an intuitive affirmation
of Swedenborg's accounts of the world beyond dying.

Part II
Preparation ～

T he more we know about the future, the better we can prepare for it. So we may find that our greatest value in knowing about the way we live after dying lies in the guidance it gives us for living now. The priorities, values, and attitudes that we adopt; the motives, intentions, and decisions we choose; the actions we take and refrain from taking—all the options from which we select a pattern in our living affect both our experience of living now and the quality of the life we will live beyond our dying. Their effect is even more conspicuous after dying when the consequences of our existential situation and various external aspects of our living no longer cloud our perception.

Preparing for our future is not easy. It requires concentration and effort; we must reject many short-term values and transitory pleasures in favor of longer-range goals. But there are clear and "do-able" steps to take, a complete "self-help program" that leads to a better life in this world and prepares us for our future beyond dying. It involves choosing a new direction for ourselves, turning around, changing ourselves, and becoming new.

Luke 12:34 "Wherever your treasure lies, there your heart will be."

6

Becoming What We Choose

The kind of life we will live after dying is a product of the life we are living now. It is a consequence of our decisions and actions, our attitudes and purposes. In addition, the kind of transition we experience between these phases of living—that is, the way we die—is significantly affected by the way we have been living and by how we understand and feel about living. A primary benefit that can be derived from knowing about how living continues after dying is the incentive to change our way of life to make it a better preparation for the transition and continuation of living.

An unprejudiced analysis of the life we have been living will indicate a strong tendency to develop into the kind of person we most want to be and to live the kind of life we most want to live. It is a tendency rather than an accomplishment, because each of us enters life with a limited range of possibilities and prospects. We have the inner freedom to choose our own direction, but a variety of external restraints—social, economic, cultural, educational, genetic, and geographical factors—limit our range of actual accomplishment. Also, the direction of development is the one we want most and have chosen in preference to others that we also desire, but desire less frequently or less intensely than we do our dominant choice.

This is our situation, whether we have made our choices deliberately and with full awareness of their consequences or whether we have made them carelessly, without thinking, acting on impulse. Sometimes we simply follow the path of least resistance in a myriad of major and minor decisions made in the course of daily living. Either way—purposefully or absentmindedly—we shape and harden the dominant pattern of preferences that Swedenborg calls our "life's love" in everything we do and everything we choose not to do.

A Hitler, loving power above all else; a Mother Teresa loving compassion; an Einstein, loving abstract knowledge; a Bruce Jenner, loving physical fitness and prowess: all illustrate a love that dominates a life enough to characterize and identify it. For the vast majority of us, however, the choice is more complex and subtle, and the result is less conspicuous in our physical living. Almost every man who is a husband and a father loves to be loved, loves security for himself and his family, loves to have people do what he wants them to do, and loves for his children to grow into independent and capable adulthood. In practice, however, these desires are not pursued with equal intensity and clarity of purpose. If loving to be loved dominates, he may give gifts and favors in ways that undermine his children's independence and values. If security becomes confused with wealth, he may deprive both wife and children of emotional support and companionship while he works day and night getting money. If his love of guiding deforms into a love of controlling, he may become a dominating or even an abusive spouse and parent. It is when love for his children's growth—loving what is best for them—dominates his living that he is the best father. However, the man would look the same to his next-door neighbor, whichever love were dominant.

Understanding this condition of human life is one of

the more important tasks of living. It is a principal require-
ment for arranging our living before dying in ways that will
improve the quality of our living after dying. If the
significance of freedom of choice is understood deeply
enough to affect our system of values and pattern of preferences, it can have a great and beneficial effect on our experience of transition. That is, the kind of death we
experience is shaped by our expectations and by the way we
feel about our memories of living.

That unprejudiced analysis just mentioned also reveals
to almost everyone that the life we are living is not exactly
the one we would choose if we had some of our decisions
to make over again. Many decisions are made in response to
desires and values that are less than our highest or best, and
maybe even opposed to our overall dominant goal—our
life's love. Living with the freedom to make our own
choices (and to assume the consequent responsibility for
them) includes the possibility of this kind of lapse from our
normal practice, this kind of failure to achieve our highest
goals. Also, after we have developed a new and higher standard for ourselves, old habits will reappear in the form of
responses that used to be normal for us but appear now as
aberrations or mistakes that we regret.

Many people find themselves in this position, the circumstance described so well by the apostle Paul in Romans
7:15 as not doing what we want to do and doing what we *the human condition*
really hate. The universality of this inner contradiction has
troubled thinkers for centuries, leading them to speculate on
the origin of such behavior, particularly the selfish and destructive forms of it we call sin.

Issues surrounding the origin of sin (or original sin) are
replete with contradictions to experience and raise meta-
physical problems that would lead us astray from the present

point—how to live as we most want to live. Swedenborg discusses this situation in depth in *Divine Love and Wisdom*; but for now, it is enough to observe that most of us fall short of our highest goals and best purposes. Whatever the conditions in which we were born and raised and live now, we are alienated to some degree—alienated from God, from other people, and from ourselves. It is not necessary to explain why, and that is fortunate. Some of history's ablest thinkers have devoted their lives to trying, without clear-cut success. As Paul Tillich said, "It is a story to be told, not a proposition to be explained." Recognizing that situation, we would like to live better lives than we are living, if we had the choice. We *do* have that choice. The issue is how do we become what we choose.

The human condition [handwritten margin note]

A lifelong process ~ *The Spiritual Journey* [handwritten]

One thing to be understood is that implementing that choice is a lifelong process. The decision as to our overall direction may be made in a moment (although a moment at the culmination of other processes of direction-finding and decision-making), but every new set of circumstances requires a new interpretation of our original intention. New options continually present fresh challenges, demanding that the choice be modified or reaffirmed. Each of these interpretations, modifications, or reaffirmations creates a new starting point, a new situation from which to face the next change or challenge. Life is a process of development: in every moment, we are making and acting out choices, and we are continually becoming the cumulative consequence of those intentional actions.

With the help of God's grace [handwritten margin note]

This truth is significant for the practice of living as well as for an understanding of life, but it is not too abstract or difficult to visualize. It was illustrated to me repeatedly during my early years as a student in Boston. In this area, "rotaries" or "circles" are common features of what, for some reason, is called "traffic control." For example, a decision to travel from a northeast suburb to the airport via Route 1A is a choice that leads not to the airport, but to another range of choices. There is a point at which Route 1A is transformed from a straight road headed more or less southward, into a circle of pavement leading past a variety of radial exits, each requiring a new decision. Two of the radii promise to lead to the airport, among other places. Two more offer a variety of destinations, and one beckons a return to where the driver came from—forgetting the whole thing. This method of controlling traffic seemed to deprive me of control over my destination, particularly in fast and heavy traffic on a rainy night. I finally learned to get where I wanted to go by concentrating on the process, as well as the goal. I used the left (or inner) lane of the circle as a holding pattern until I had a chance to see all the choices available, choose among them, and then work my way into the lane from which I could act upon my decision.

Actually, one of the exits labeled "Airport" led first to another rotary. Life is like that. Choices made often lead to choices pending. Reaching a goal is the consequence of a series of choices—some in the right direction, some leading to unexpected consequences. The cumulative effect of the whole series of decisions determines the final outcome.

This is both the good news and the bad news about the lifelong process of becoming what we choose. It is good news, because past mistakes and failures need not preclude success in reaching a goal that is newly chosen, and continuing pursuit of our goal does not have to be perfect if it is persistent. It is bad news if we expect our decisions automatically to be accomplishments, or conversion to constitute instant salvation. Decisions about the overall course, or final goal, of our process of living take a lifetime to carry out. Choosing what we want to be begins a new phase of that process, and becoming what we choose takes the remaining portion of the process of living in our body.

Constructive Motivation (Motivated freely by
A self-directed process ~ ("This is what I want to do."

There is another aspect to the process that might seem like both good and bad news. The good news is that no one can force you do it. The bad news is that if it is going to happen, *you* have to force yourself. Other people can force you to do things, but what you want to do (or, in constrained or coercive situations, what you *want* to want to do) is by definition a choice that no person or institution or rule forces upon you. Freely made choices that no one forces upon you are decisions that affect the way you live after dying. In fact, those choices—especially the ones you put into action—make all the difference in the kind of living you will do then. Nothing else has very much effect at all.

Everything about your living after you die is determined by the choices you make now and in the rest of your physical living. The community you live in will comprise spirits who made choices like yours during their physical living. The kind of work you do then will be a spiritual equivalent or extension of what you most enjoy doing now. The home you live in, the clothes you wear, your posture and your stature, all will be functions then of your particular pattern of choices and preferences made now.

Also, and for the same reasons, the attitudes and expectations with which you enter the process of dying are the same attitudes and expectations that you have now, or that you may develop before you do begin that process. A cliché common during World War II reflected a popular denial of this fact. "There are no atheists in foxholes" suggested that proximity to death with bullets whining overhead and artillery shells bursting all around would force skeptical soldiers to believe in God and in living beyond dying. Later reflection on their experiences, however, showed that fear of dying induced fervent hopes for a protecting God and a peaceful heaven, but faith or trust was experienced only by those who had formed their convictions earlier. A physician's prognosis that death is imminent may induce the same hopes in a patient as bombs and bullets do in soldiers, but the kind of confidence that brings comfort in the time of dying must be developed while we have the freedom from fear that allows uncoerced conviction.

The life you have been living has a great influence on your choice of a new direction. It is said that the leaf does not fall far from the tree, and it is true that choosing a new direction somewhat similar to your present one is easier than choosing a radically different one. Swedenborg notes:

Patterns of Living ~

It is known that habit is a second nature, and that therefore what is easy for one is difficult for another; and this is true of self-examination and a confession of what is thereby discovered. What is easier for a hired laborer, a porter, or a farmer than to work with his hands from morning till evening, while a gentleman or a delicate person could not do the same work for half an hour without fatigue and sweating? It is easy for a footman with a staff and easy boots to pursue his way for miles, while one accustomed to ride can hardly run slowly from one street to another. Every mechanic who is attentive to his task goes through it easily and willingly, and when he leaves it, longs to return; while another, who understands the same trade, but is indolent, can scarcely be driven to work. The same is true of every one, whatever may be his office or pursuit. To one diligent in piety, what is easier than to pray to God? While to one who is a slave to impiety, what is more difficult, and vice versa? What priest, preaching before a king for the first time, does not feel timid, but after doing it frequently goes through boldly? What is easier for an angelic man than to raise his eyes to heaven, or for a devilish man than to cast them down toward hell? But if the latter becomes a hypocrite, he too can look up to heaven, but his heart is turned away. Every one becomes imbued with the end he has in view and the habit arising therefrom.

True Christian Religion 563

∽

The direction, or goal, that we choose now—and work to achieve—is crucially important for the way in which we will die, and for the kind of living we will experience beyond that great transition. Its significance is not limited to the future, however, because the quality of our living now is affected just as strongly—and even more directly and immediately—by the direction in which we choose to develop. The same purposes and values that lead to heavenly living beyond dying and enhance our ability to face death with confidence and composure also make day-to-day living more rewarding and more manageable.

Intentions that harmonize with those of angels prepare us to join their heavenly community—and gain the support and guidance of those angels—as well as lending us some of the joy in the work that they experience continually and fully.

The responsibility placed upon us by our freedom to choose our own direction is awesome, in the true sense of that word. Our satisfaction today, our certainty at our time for dying, and the quality of our life beyond physical death hinge on our own free choice of which values and purposes guide our living.

In humility, choose God's grace.

7

Turning Around

There is nothing better than God's Will. God's Will is love and the Best of the very Best for each and everyone of us—happiness and fulfillment for all.

T he lifelong process of becoming what we choose is already underway, of course. It is more or less advanced depending on our age, the kind of life we have been living, and the degree to which intention or accident has affected its course. Beginning a process of becoming what we now choose, in place of what we had chosen before, involves three steps. They are closely connected, but each must be distinguished if it is to be accomplished. The first step in turning around is recognizing that our primary goal—our life's love, the purpose that has focused and guided our life up until now—is not the one we really want. There is something better. Second, we must choose a life goal that meets our higher criteria. And third, we need to will, to intend, that goal—adopt it, make it our own life's love—by taking concrete action toward its implementation.

All three phases are essential. Without any one of them, the effort to fulfill the new vision for our life is misdirected or aborted. If we do not abandon our old purpose completely and decisively, our election of a new one will be diluted and uncertain. It will fail at the first hard choice between our new love and our old one. If we reject our former goal but do not clearly envision and firmly choose a

Visualize and affirm our new and higher goals.

63

new one, our higher purpose <u>will not be vivid or solid enough to</u> hold us in a really difficult situation. Even if we are precise and determined in these things, <u>nothing is accomplished until</u> (we take action,) doing something that moves toward realization of our intention. *Taking steps*

Together, these three phases make up the first step toward a new kind of living. It can be called changing direction. It is described as a first step in life-changing programs in many traditions. In biblical language, it is called repentance; but that term is frequently misunderstood as meaning regret, or feeling sorry. Although you may have regrets at the time you are ready to repent, *repentance* actually means <u>"turning around," as in changing direction.</u> Repentance is a complete reorientation. If you are looking for a street address, such as 3150 Somewhere Lane, and you pass houses marked 3210, 3230, and 3250, repentance will be necessary to get you to your destination. That does not mean feeling sorry that the addresses are wrong. It means turning around, going the other way, changing direction.

Changing direction, by itself, is not enough to get you to your goal, either. It is necessary, but it is not sufficient. When you are going the wrong way, no amount of effort will get you where you want to be unless you change course. <u>But after turning around, you have to walk. It may be that a journey of a thousand miles starts with a single step, but only if that first step is a step in the right direction, and only if it is taken. Because the process is self-directed, you must choose the goal, you must turn yourself around, and you must take that first step in the right direction.</u>

Checking the compass ∾

Turning toward the right direction requires knowing which direction is right for you. Probably no one ever woke up one morning and decided that today, and for the rest of his or her life, he is going to move in the wrong direction. No one says, "Today, I will develop my evil tendencies and preferences as diligently as I can." Rather, most of us live our days trying to keep up with what has to be done, not devoting a lot of attention to questions of good and evil or to the overall direction of our life.

I'm busy. I do my job, pay my bills, buy the groceries, cut the grass and shovel the sidewalks, and, like, vote. Right?

Yes, right, so far.

And, besides, the main thing about "right and wrong" is that I've got a "right" to keep anyone from "doing me wrong." If I don't look out for number one, who will? After all, life doesn't come with a user's manual, so we have to make it up as we go along, and just make sure that if anyone gets hurt, it isn't me. Right?

No, not right. Wrong.

All the religions of the world offer a "user's' manual" for life, and cultural mores provide guidance for behavior that meets a higher ethical standard than merely "looking out for number one." The world's most widely used financial instrument affirms "In God We Trust," but the world's daily business depends on trust in people—faith that people will maintain ethical standards.

It was a few months before I was to start kindergarten, when America's banks closed and the economy came to a grinding and painful halt; but I vividly recall two events that draw from that extreme circumstance, something central to the business of business and the business of life.

A few hours before the banks closed in 1929, but on the

same day, a St. Louis businessman with whom my father had frequent dealings, a William Baggerman, wrote a check for something like $500 and paid a bill with it. Almost six weeks elapsed before that check returned to his bank (which had long-since reopened). It had so many endorsements that they covered the back of the check plus several pieces of paper stapled to it. Tens of thousands of dollars worth of bills had been paid with that stapled string of paper scraps attached to a promise that Mr. Baggerman would pay $500. As my father explained, repeating the story to enough people that I still remember it more than six decades later, "everyone knew that Mr. Baggerman's promise would be good, no matter what happened to the banks." So, what paid all those bills? It wasn't money, because that was locked up in the banks. It was people's trust in William Baggerman that paid the bills. And, although the trust is better-secured in most cases, it is trust that keeps the economy working—trust that people live by higher principles than looking out for number one.

A smaller lesson was played out for me a few months later. Dad, who was a real estate agent, had lost the house he was buying, and our family had moved into a house offered by a client until money freed up a little and Dad could find a buyer. Our groceries, as well as our shelter, was provided at times by the same principle. I recall my father asking a grocer, "Can you give me a little food on credit?" "Might as well," he replied. "I'd rather go broke from people owing me money, than from not doing any business." We bought food with trust, and later paid for the trust in cash.

The Great Depression provides numerous examples of the trust that underlies our daily living. But we need not go back that far. Today, driving down the street, we trust without thinking that drivers coming toward us will stay in their lane, and drivers at stop-signs will stay there until we have crossed in front of them. We trust that their mechanics and ours repaired the cars to make them safe. We trust that pilots and air controllers have the self-discipline to stay away from alcohol and other drugs before they take charge of our safety. There are countless examples of the unconsidered but fundamental expectation that people around us live by principles that are at least similar to the principles of the great religions, such as the "Golden Rule"—so called because of its common currency in so many religious and ethical traditions: *Act toward others as you want them to act toward you.*

These illustrations serve only to establish a kind of minimal basis for confirming the existence of an almost universally recognized standard or norm for behavior. This basic, no-frills minimum is sometimes called "enlightened selfishness"; but the "light" in that formulation radiates from something like John Stewart Mills' utilitarian principle of "the greatest good for the greatest number," if it is not in fact derived from altruistic humanism or from religion itself.

The conclusion is defensible, if not inescapable: there are standards, norms, guiding principles available to everyone, accessible by everyone, recognizable by everyone, and acceptable to almost everyone. There are fixed poles in our mental and moral universe, and there are compasses by which we can check our bearings. We can, if we want to, determine if the direction of our current life-path is a good one. We can find road maps to better destinations.

Emanuel Swedenborg's literary road maps to the kind of living that leads to heavenly life are based on the Bible as both poles and compass for living in this world. The experience I have had in my cultural circumstances leads to solid confirmation of that same "lamp for my feet and light for my path" (Psalms 119:105) But it is plain to me—as it was to Swedenborg, when he saw heavenly living available to those who achieve the standards of all religions—that many religions and traditions offer the kind of guidance needed to make the right choices and begin growing in the right direction. The responsibility of finding, and taking, the right path is ours; but there is no excuse for not knowing the way. There are enough signposts for everyone to find his or her own direction, regardless of cultural heritage or religious preference.

Changing directions ∾

Turning ourselves around is more easily said than done. No step in the whole process is harder. The path we have been on is familiar, whatever we now think is wrong with it, and changing direction is ominous if not frightening. At least some of our friends are still following that path, and it is difficult to break away from them. Our friends do not make it easy for us: they see us as abandoning purposes that once were shared, and as rejecting *them*. In fact, we may *have to* reject our old friends if they will not reject their old goals and values and adopt new ones like ours. Maintaining their friendship leaves us vulnerable to dangerously seductive influences from our former preferences and intentions. *If you don't want a haircut, stay out of the barber shop.*

Turning around is difficult, but help is available. Whatever guide or compass we used to choose our new direction will offer further guidance in staying on the new path. If the Bible is your guide, it can be a staff to lean on, too: it offers many resources of strength and encouragement for walking in its light. If you have found your new direction with the help of a priest, pastor, or rabbi; or if you are a member of a twelve-step self-help organization, a church, or other spiritually oriented group, you have access to experienced, compassionate, and powerful help in holding to your new course. Far more people succeed at following a new way of living if they do it with the help of a support system. Seek out the help, and make all the use of it you can. Turning around is hard enough. You will need all the help you can get. There are no "extra points" for going it alone. The prize is in succeeding, and it is no less precious for your having had help along the way.

Some changes of direction are easier to make and maintain than others. Perhaps it is contrary to inexperienced expectation, but a radical change may well be made more easily than a slight or subtle change. People who have been addicted to alcohol, or other drugs, or to compulsive gambling, can—at great emotional cost, to be sure—isolate themselves from opportunities to engage in the behavior they have decided to reject. As wrenching as this may be, many find it easier to handle than the plight of, for instance, compulsive overeaters who must taste their tempter several times a day. Restraining may be more difficult than quitting. The alcoholic in recovery had to quit once, but the overeater has to quit eating at every meal.

On the other hand, changes of direction involving restraint, while continuing some aspects of former practices, have the advantage of retaining more that is desirable about the familiar way of living, and so may be easier in some ways than complete reversals of course that require massive and upsetting changes in lifestyle.

The important thing about turning around is to do it. Nothing about the process is made easier by delay or by equivocation. Quitting drinking is hard, but quitting for the third time (or the fifth, or the twentieth) is progressively harder still. It may be easier to taper off your use of nicotine by using a medically controlled "patch" than to quit smoking cold-turkey, but the *decision* to quit—the mental, emotional, and spiritual turning around—must be made decisively if the patch or other treatment is to work. Nike's ad campaign "Just do it" and Nancy Reagan's anti-drug slogan "Just say no" have two things in common. Both are immeasurably harder to carry out than to say. And both are immeasurably better than messing around.

8 ～
Changing the Self

L iving in a better way than we have been living is work. It is hard work, because of the concentration, discipline, and effort involved. It is not endlessly difficult, however. The nature of the process includes a development in which the new way of living is no longer new, but is the natural and characteristic pattern of responses to life until the new way of life becomes *our* way of life. That final stage is the subject of the next chapter, but it needs to be mentioned here so that the work of changing is not mistaken for an endlessly repetitive labor. Changing our way of life is a job of work, a task with an achievable goal.

Each change affects a specific area or aspect of living, and a major change in life direction involves working on many changes at once. Each change, when it becomes established in our life, creates the possibility of further change, based on new capabilities that grow out of the change. The completion of one task, therefore, is the beginning of another in a complex process of ongoing development. In this respect, the work of living in a better way is an unending work. It should not, nevertheless, be confused with the labor of Sisyphus, who was condemned to roll a great rock up a hill, only to have it roll back to the bottom every time it neared the top. Sisyphus had to start over from the same beginning point every time he approached the summit; but the work of changing our life starts over at a new point, a new beginning, as we complete each phase of our development. With each beginning, the possibilities and the goal are higher and more worth the effort.

It must be added that changing human nature's many interconnected aspects requires developing many strands of character at the same time, without all aspects changing at the same rate. Changing a way of living involves a number of cycles of change proceeding at varying rates of growth in a complex, multi-threaded development. It is easier to understand than to describe, because we are so familiar with it. Human life itself is just such a chaotic, tumultuously complex process.

Forcing the self ⌇

When we embark on a process of intentional change, it is as if we divide our self into two opposing teams. Both are recruited from within us, are parts of our being; but only the victor becomes part of our nature, our character, our *self*, that emerges changed from the struggle. One team takes a role much like the offensive team in a football game and tries to bring about the change while the other defends the status quo *against* change. Like an offensive squad in football, the part of us that wants to change usually runs "set plays" (often "called in" by self-help literature, a twelve-step group, friends in a congregation, or a professional counselor, much as plays are given to a quarterback from an offensive coordinator above the press box). Our conservative side, like a defensive squad, is more creative and flexible, responding to every offensive effort in the way most likely to resist the change.

Program your subconcious by visualizing. seeing yourself with the change already accomplished. See it, Feel it, hear it, smell it, taste it as accomplished in the Present Moment.

Changing the Self

This defensive squad is particularly effective against the "long bomb" and "end runs." "Hail Mary" passes or long sideline dashes seldom work, because our inner resistance to change is especially alert to that kind of play and rarely gives up big yardage to dramatic showboat tactics. <u>The surest way to overcome our own resistance to change is an in-your-face, up-the-middle game plan that grinds out four yards in a cloud of dust, play after play, until it crosses the "goal line" and becomes our characteristic life pattern. There is no reliable shortcut to self-change.</u> *Also, use Affirmations of change already accomplished*

The clashing struggle of large bodies at the line of scrimmage is an apt image for the intense and many-faceted effort to force our self to change. The offense and defense are equally matched, of course: as the cartoon character Pogo once announced from the comic page, both sides are us. Having one part of our mind accept a change while the other opposes it is a familiar scenario in our life. Recall a time when you "forced yourself" to get out of bed in the morning, "made yourself" finish a task when you were tired or hungry or bored, "really had to argue with yourself" about keeping an obligation: the "other side" is formidable, and success is by no means assured.

Another illustration of the process—the one most frequently found in the Bible and the favorite of Emanuel Swedenborg—is the image of a battle. It may be more appropriate than football, at least for the reason that football is only a game (*pace* college bowl and Super Bowl fans); and war, like the changing of our lives, is a matter of life and death. It is important to remember the significance of this struggle, because—as has been pointed out—by the time its seriousness becomes inescapably obvious (with the imminent approach of your own or a close loved one's death), the war may be over. The battle may be lost.

On the other hand, the football image has the advantage of playing out the cyclical nature of the struggle to change our self. After victory or loss in a specific area of change (after each touchdown or turnover), the play resumes. With each new beginning (each kickoff or punt), the struggle continues from the new starting point (the score) attained by earlier efforts.

Whatever image you visualize, the equality of the two sides must be kept in mind. Your resistance to changing your self has all the same mental abilities, the same knowledge of which "buttons" to push for maximum effect, and the same capacity for rationalization, as your determination to change. This inescapable balance of forces means that your determination to change will need reinforcements if it is to succeed. The Bible is such a resource, as are other religious texts and works that can serve as compass and staff for this undertaking. A minister or counselor can help a lot if you describe the difficulties you are having soon enough for the counsel to be useful. If you are working at change in the context of a group of people who are changing themselves, talk to the members frankly and often. Especially in the case of working with a self-help group, discussing the problems and accomplishments of self-change is necessary for your progress, and for the group's as well: every exchange of experience and advice helps the giver as well as the recipient—and all who hear it, as well.

Working against the grain ∿

After committing to a new direction, the work we do in changing our essential self includes forcing ourselves to do unfamiliar, even awkward things—or, do the same old

74 ∿

[handwritten annotation: Visualize vividly in detail what you want. See, hear, feel, smell and taste what you want to Program the subconscious mind.]

things in what may feel to be an unfamiliar or awkward way. The same process works in many areas of self-change, whether we are changing the moral direction of our life, or improving our dexterity and skill at work, in a sport, or an artistic endeavor. Hammering a nail, using a keyboard, swinging a bat or a golf club, fingering piano keys, blending watercolors, and many other techniques are mastered only by the same kind of change in our self that is required for changing the way we live. In both categories of change, our natural, instinctive, subconscious actions and reactions must be altered. One implication of this fact is that our hidden nature—the subconscious levels of our mind, the compulsion of our instinctual tendencies—rebels against the instructions of our conscious mind. *[handwritten: program the subconscious]*

[handwritten right margin: mind with what you want. Visualize it.]

These hidden aspects of our personality are powerful opponents in the struggle to change our self, but they have an Achilles' heel. If our conscious determination compels them to do a new and unfamiliar thing repeatedly and consistently, they eventually adopt the new way as the natural and instinctive way our subconscious operates. When that happens, they rebel against the old way as stubbornly as, at first, they fought against the new way. Reaching that point requires steady discipline at doing things in a way that feels wrong, going against the grain, until, in effect, the grain changes.

Professor Coleman Bender, of Emerson College in Boston, used to describe the process of self-change in four steps. The first he called "unconscious incompetence" because, at that stage, you are doing whatever it is you are doing wrong but don't even know it is wrong. Holding a golf club with the wrong grip, thus creating an unwanted tendency to slice, is an example of unconscious incompetence. His second step was "conscious incompetence"; this stage, induced by a teacher, or perhaps by careful observation of your own swing and that of others, involves the recognition that a better grip on the club might improve your game. Bender's third stage, "conscious competence," refers to the disciplined struggle under discussion here. It is the stage in which you grip the club properly and hit the ball straighter, but only when you concentrate on doing it the way you have been taught. The new way feels uncomfortable, awkward, as if it should not work; but as long as you force yourself to do it anyway, the ball goes closer to where you aimed it. This is the hard phase in changing yourself. The next and last stage, "unconscious competence," is the one in which you automatically grip the club properly, without thinking, whenever you pick it up and the ball continues to fly straight.

St. Paul: Pursue Love as the greatest wisdom of all.

We are created in the image and likeness of God. Becoming new is with the help of God's grace manifesting the divine imprint within us.

9

Becoming New: *Becoming love.*

"change toward being more loving is the best change we can make in ourselves." p 79

After examining our self in the light of a higher standard, after making a choice and a commitment, after forcing our self to go against the grain and do what we have decided instead of what has become familiar and comfortable—after all that, our hope is to become a new person. In fact, becoming the person we have chosen to be, instead of the person we were, is to become a person who lives, but—in one sense, at least—had not lived before. It is to become what the apostle Paul called "a new creation."

Christians often call this process being "born again." Emanuel Swedenborg adopted the same terminology, but gave it such a specific meaning that his translators have consistently kept the original Latin term *regeneratio* in English editions, calling it "regeneration." Swedenborg uses "regeneration" to describe the entire process of becoming new, as well as the final stage of each cycle in the process and the goal of the process. "Becoming new" is a free rendering of Swedenborg's meaning, denoting a process of self-examination, free choice, and self-directed transformation that results in becoming a new person and living in a new way. He uses the same term for the third stage of the whole process— "becoming new" after "turning around" and "trying our best"—and for the goal of the life-long process. Being regenerated, becoming new, being born again—this is the way, the only way, to heavenly living.

Becoming new is the way to live in our body in this world, so as to live better after dying, and so as to arrive better prepared at the time for our dying, or the time of someone very close to us. It is the reason for thinking about the reality of living beyond dying, and for examining the process of dying, so that the long-term and short-term reasons for becoming new can be established.

If dying, and living beyond dying, presents us with questions, the answers are offered in the process of becoming new. Complete answers are not to be found in any list of specific things to *do*—still less in any list of prohibitions—because the context of any action or denial determines its consequence in our life. Nels Ferre, professor of theology at Vanderbilt University and Andover Newton Theological School, liked to remind his classes that there is no list of things you can *not do* to be a Christian, because you have to *do* something to be worthy of that label. But it is also true that you have to do the right things *and* avoid doing the wrong things *for the right reasons.*

Becoming new means becoming a person who loves doing good things simply because they are good and hates doing bad things because they are bad, and is unconcerned in either case with reputation, reward, or advantage. It is becoming the kind of person who lives by the advice of a north African who, fifteen centuries ago, chose a new direction, changed himself, and truly became new (and eventually became a bishop, as well). His name was Augustine. Changed from a strongly anti-Christian philosopher, mainly by the pleas of his mother and what he believed was divine intervention, Augustine became one of Christianity's greatest theologians. He wrote, on the basis of his beliefs and his own

Loving: Wanting the Best for others

Loving truly the way God loves ←

experience, "Love [God and your neighbors], and then do whatever you want to do [as an expression of your love.]"

In the context of Augustine's extensive writings, that advice is deceptively simple, but it points to two fundamental truths about the work of changing our self. The first is that, for change to be durable and significant, it must go beyond a change in what we do and include a change in our motivation, a change in the reasons that we do what we do. It is only when loving—wanting the best for others—is our motivation, that anything we want to do will be loving and therefore good for others. The second great truth is that change is good only if it is in a good direction, and change toward being more loving is the best change we can make in ourselves.

The idea of loving—living with love as our dominant motive—needs clarification because the word *love* is abused, overused, and often misunderstood. The oldest New Testament texts we know were written in Greek, so Paul and the gospel writers had three words to express three different kinds of love. There was *philia*, which referred to deep friendship, the kind of love that is common between siblings. There was *eros*, the passionate and possessive kind of love that includes sexual attraction. Finally, there was *agápe*, selflessly desiring good for others—*agápe* in its supreme form, describing the very nature of God. That linguistic abundance allowed a precision in the gospel statements about love that is hard to duplicate in English. Modern slang, in addition, has heaped new meanings upon the word *love*. When a teenaged girl "loves" a pair of shoes because "they're to die for," and people "make love" with someone they have known for only a couple of hours and do not expect to see again, Augustine's advice could mean almost anything. Or nothing.

Part II: Preparation

As the word is used by Augustine and in this chapter, love is not something we do, have, make, or fall into. Love is our life. We are what we love doing. We *really* are what we *most* love doing. Swedenborg compares love in people's lives to the warmth of the sun in the life of plants:

⁓

The sun's warmth . . . is, so to speak, the shared life of all earth's plants, since when it increases—as happens in springtime—all kinds of plants spring up from the soil. They deck themselves with leaves, then with blossoms, and finally with fruits.

Divine Love and Wisdom 3

⁓

Everything we think, say, or do is the direct consequence of our wanting, desiring, loving. But the nature of this loving is determined by its object. If we love ourselves, that makes one kind of living. If we love the world around us and the things in it, that is another kind of loving and makes a different kind of life. If we love the people who are close to us—physically and spiritually close—or if we love all people as children of God, that is something else again. Finally, there is the possibility of living a life in which every intention flows from our loving the Lord.

In practice, most of us are motivated by all four of these loves, but inevitably we prioritize them. When we are engaged in religious rites and sacraments, we feel a love toward God; but if our engagement is motivated in part by a desire to be seen and admired as a religious person, then we are loving God for the sake of our love for ourselves. We may do good things for other people; but if we do them so that we will be admired for our kindness, then we are loving others for the sake of our love for ourselves.

Those are two of the possible perversions of the good love that we experience as a result of changing ourselves in the right direction. The goal of this work is loving: loving ourselves, indeed, but loving ourselves for the sake of the world and others in it; and loving others and the world for the sake of—as an expression of—our love for God. When our motives are prioritized in that order, we are capable of receiving love from God and radiating it to all around us in the most exciting and satisfying life that can be imagined. That kind of living is a gift. It is a gift that God offers to all, but this gift can be received only by those who have changed their loving into the right priorities.

Gift of God ~ God's grace

Inherent in this whole discussion of becoming new is the assumption that we cannot make ourselves new. Becoming new is a gift. Many call it the gift of grace. Whatever it is called, it must be recognized as a gift from God, from a power greater than our self, an accomplishment we cannot achieve on our own. There is a philosophical question as to whether any human being can do anything by his or her power alone; but that need not be settled here. The unquestionable certainty is that we cannot lift ourselves off the ground by pulling on our own bootstraps. By our own will, we cannot make our essential self become a new person.

We can choose a direction, we can commit our self to working toward it, we can change our behavior. We can persist in behavioral change long enough for it to become habitual. But we cannot *make* it habitual, and we cannot

It is God (God's love and grace) that transforms us, that makes us a new creation. Thanks be to God!

force our self to want what we have decided in principle that we want to want. That final step in the process, that transformation of *acting* differently into *becoming* different and new, that final and decisive change is a gift. It cannot be given to us before we have done the work of preparing for it, but that is different from thinking that we earn it or bring it about by our own effort. Effort—a *lot* of diligent effort—is necessary, but not sufficient, for becoming new.

In one formulation and context or another, that is a central teaching of Christianity and the world's major religions, and of the twelve-step tradition of self-help programs as well. It is important to remember for at least two reasons. One reason is the encouragement it offers. When the effort of changing seems overwhelming, it is helps a lot to remember that we are not in this battle alone. If we do our part *as if* we were on our own, God's loving action will help us, and eventually put us over the top. The same principle guards against short-circuiting the process by overestimating our part in it. Doing our part consistently and patiently will bring our efforts to change our self to the point at which the gift is given as we become new. If, instead, we persist only as long as we think is necessary, our natural defense against change may fool us so it will not be long enough, and the process will not work.

Becoming new is a life-long process that we experience in many cycles occurring in different aspects of our lives. It does not happen in one great flash with a trumpet crash, with our new self unrecognizably different from our self of a moment ago. Various changes occur, most of them small in themselves, few of them recognized even by us until sometime after they occur. Perhaps, in a reflective moment after an accomplishment, we realize that we could not have done that at some particular time in the past. Or, ruminating briefly on a small disappointment, we will recall that the same sort of thing used to get us really upset.

This gift of unconscious competence to replace the awkward diligence of conscious competence is not *earned* by an indentured period of servitude to the discipline of self-change. It is freely given according to an observed law of *God's grace* living that does not have to be understood to be experienced. Indeed, it does not even have to be believed to be experienced. Becoming new follows the work of changing our self with the dependability of sunrise and gravity, just as light dawns and apples fall on the learned and the simple, the faithful and the doubting. ✓

A new creation ∿

The result of this process is not an accomplishment or the end of anything. It is more of a transition or a new beginning. It is finding our self to be a new creation, starting at a point from which a new goal can be seen and a new effort of self-change can be begun. It is a high point in a cyclical process, as when a bicycle pedal is at the top of its circle and ready to begin another rotation while moving forward with the whole bicycle.

Growing while we live is like that. We keep working at what appear to be the same problems, while both we and the problems continue to change a little at a time. Once in a while, we notice the feeling of being at the top and enjoy it, before plunging into the process again. Sometimes we can coast at the top for a while, feeling some satisfaction in our progress; but the moment passes (just as the dark moments at the bottom of the cycle do), and the work goes on.

Even dying turns out to be another transition in the

long, cyclical process of change. When our body can no longer serve our spirit in the process, the new creation we have become in this physical life becomes the starting point for our spiritual growth in the new kind of life that is living beyond dying.

If we have done well in the ongoing cyclical struggle, we will approach the time of dying as an active participant in a number of concentric and interconnected communities—physical ones as well as spiritual. We will find our communal goals taking up more of our attention and energy than our purely individual ones, although that distinction will be less clear than it once was. Our personal goals, selected in the context of our common commitments, will be close to or will overlap the goals of one or more of the spiritual heavenly or hellish groups in which we participate.

Being involved with a community may not require us to be physically close to people at the time. A writer who is writing, for example, usually is alone (or attempting to block out awareness of other people who may be present) but is actively involved with several communities. There is a spiritual community whose members enjoy discussing the subject on which he or she is writing, and perhaps another that occupies itself with influencing others in the direction that the writer is trying to influence readers. Because time affects spiritual interactions differently from physical ones, there is spiritual involvement with those who will read what is written after it is published. Also, there is spiritual involvement with people in his or her physical community— those who help protect the author's time and opportunity to write, those who are waiting for the manuscript, perhaps to edit it, and other people as well. We always are involved with a circle of people, spirits and communities, whatever we do. Our choice of purpose determines which communities are involved with us.

When we are among people, either face-to-face or communicating by phone or e-mail or whatever, we will find that the new creation we have become is concerned about them more than about ourselves. The more we have to do with them, the more we will try to make their interaction with us today a satisfying one, cheerful and encouraging, so that their day is better for having dealt with us. When we see people in need—in need of help of any kind, or of support or advice or counsel, or even a hug (if we are genuine about it)—we will find joy and fulfillment in responding to that need.

We pay our taxes, work for causes, study issues, and vote in elections. We obey traffic signs and speed limits, and in countless details of modern living we try to do what is good for the larger and smaller circles of community in which we operate. Being new creations, we do these things because we want to do them. They are expressions of our love for our neighbors, and that love is, in turn, an expression of our love for God. Everything we do because we love becomes a source of quiet joy.

Once in a while, a very few of us have an opportunity to do something for our community that gets in the newspapers or on the evening news; but mostly we live lives of quiet accomplishment. Our particular accomplishment may be of obvious help to someone, like the ministrations of a hospice worker to a dying man and his desperate wife; or almost invisible in the vast machinery of modern society, like a keyboard operator in a skyscraper office. The prominence of the work is less important to our personal growth and the welfare of our community than the diligence and good will with which we do it.

We have fun as new creations. We smile often, and sometimes we laugh or sing for joy. We try to avoid frustrations by developing respect for ourselves and trust in our neighbors. We rely on those around us, both physically and spiritually, for companionship, and for the kind of help we are glad to give—a helping hand, a smile, advice, sympathy. shared grief, shared joy, support.

Living as a new creation is living well. Usually, it is so unspectacular as to be boring to hear about; but it also has moments of drama, success, and failure. The important thing about this living is that it benefits someone. Our community is better because of what we have done in it today.

When we come to the time for dying—our own time, or that of one close to our life and our inner self—we can face it without fear. Having learned to live to help others, we can take satisfaction in what we have become and die content. Having recognized the reality of our spiritual community, we can look forward to living its life and know that our loved ones still will be loved and still will be able to love and serve. Without lightning, thunder, or trumpets, life offers satisfactions out of its challenges, and dying offers hope out of its difficulties.

Part III
Transition ~

W hen speaking of dying as a transition, we must take care to avoid the euphemistic thinking that shies away from ideas like pain, suffering, and death itself. Believing the promise of life's continuation after death, accepting it as fact, does not dilute physical pain in the experience nor the sorrow of physical loss. Thanksgiving that a loved one's suffering has ended may balance, but not erase, the consuming loneliness in the physical consciousness of one who is left to mourn. Faith may transform grief and loneliness by changing their context, but the grief and loneliness are real. Subconscious denial of death and of consequent loss, with all the destructive psychological effects of contrary-to-fact denial, sometimes masquerades as spiritual superiority over death. Noel Coward's contempt for that kind of flight from unpleasantness stands as a wry warning against fuzzy thinking that attempts to mask feelings by changing terms. In his play *Blithe Spirit*, a character replies to the euphemism *passing over* (with a dry emphasis that probably works better on stage than in print): "She didn't pass over, pass under, or pass out. She DIED!"

Clear terminology is vital to clear thinking, and clear thinking is necessary in understanding death as a transition between two kinds of living. "Passing over" is an accurate term that describes a spirit's transition, but it should not imply that survivors' grief is any less real. Nothing said here is intended to dilute the seriousness of death, the agony that often accompanies it, the tragedy it may force upon the lives of people who love or depend on the one who dies, or its irreversible finality ("near-death" may be reversible, but death is not). The experience of dying may be frightening, painful, or worse. The dying person's discomfort may be increased by those who are closest and care the most, and when there is agony in our body's last moments, it is painful for those who care. There are negative aspects to spare when thinking about the physical experience of dying, and some of them will be considered here.

However, one truth about death is also a solace in living and dying. No one dies forever. Death is a process. Death has an end. That ending also stops forever any pain the physical body feels in the dying process and whatever pain the mind and spirit may share with loved ones for their loss. Although some may wish that it might come later than it does and some pray that it come sooner, the end does come. The spirit awakening to the new kind of living gains a new perspective that radically changes mental pain and contains nothing at all of any physical agony the body may have experienced.

10 ∿

Death Scenes

Everyone dies, but few people die in the same way. The many ways of dying and the extreme importance of the event in the lives of loving survivors emphasize the distinctiveness of each death. Stories recounted beside ceremoniously opened caskets enumerate every detail surrounding the moment of death or the discovery of the body. The precise description and its seemingly endless repetition together form a ritual of homage and help to counteract any covert tendency of survivors to deny the reality of this particular death. This emphasis on the particularity of each death makes it difficult to consider kinds or categories of ways in which people die.

Separating a spirit from a body is not a simple process. The two aspects of human living are too intertwined and interdependent to part from each other easily. While a few individuals die peacefully with no previous illness or injury—and in an ideal world more people might—living just before dying most often involves either sudden or prolonged physical pain and deterioration of mind or body (or both) that causes mental and maybe spiritual pain. Beyond this nearly universal suffering in connection with dying, two kinds of dying are different enough to preclude much discussion of both together.

Some people die suddenly within minutes or a few hours of an accident, or after the first symptoms of a brief illness, and may be unconscious for all or most of even that short time. Others die by a slower series of weakenings and failures, sometimes according to (or in defiance of) a prognostic timetable.

Catastrophic dying ↩

Men or women who die during their active adult years are most likely to die as a result of accidents, and the overwhelming majority of these fatal accidents involve automobiles. It may be logical that accidents kill more people in the prime of their lives than diseases do because, by definition, that is the period when their health is expected to be at its peak, along with their other powers. Because of that expectation, dying in the first three or four decades of living seems tragically unnatural and deprives others of help and support they had reasonably expected to depend on. Children, spouses, business partners, associates, clients, and (not least) friends, all are wounded in some way by deaths in this age group. When the dying is unpredicted and sudden—whether from an accident or from an unsuspected illness like cardiac arrest or stroke—many lives, plans, hopes and expectations are dashed in a momentary event that seems senseless and contrary to the natural order. There is bad news to be delivered; there is shock, grieving, adjustment, reordering, and many other difficult trials for survivors to endure.

When death or at least terminal unconsciousness is immediate, survivors may find some comfort in the thought their loved one did not suffer, but not all catastrophic accidents or illnesses are that clean or that kind. Mental and verbal re-creations of the event, occurring endlessly in early stages of grief, envision at least a moment of terror when the impending catastrophe is recognized—feeling the car going out of control, seeing another car on a collision course, realizing that a sudden pain actually is a heart attack—and at least another moment in which pain explodes to fill consciousness before overwhelming it.

There is evidence that this imagined end of physical living may not always reflect reality. Fifty-two years ago, I was hit by a trolley-car in what clearly could have been a fatal accident. I was left with no memory of what happened. I recall the trolley was stopped across the street, taking on passengers; I stepped off the curb to cross in front of it, and the next thing I remember is waking up on the floor of a corner bar (!) where neighbors had carried me. Similarly, I have heard a report of a climber who fell from a cliff to what might well have been his death and who remembers falling but does not remember hitting the ground. In his work *How We Die*, Sherwin Nuland relates that in some terrifying moments—for example, in a collapse from a heart attack, another could-have-been-fatal accident, and even a particularly horrific murder—the victims sometimes are spared both terror and pain by some action of brain chemistry or other mental or spiritual intervention.[4] Even in slower, attended dying, some of the death agonies that so distress bedside watchers occur after the patient has lost consciousness for the last time. These merciful suppressions of fear and pain at the moment of dying do not always

---

4. Sherwin Nuland, *How We Die* (New York: Alfred A. Knopf, 1995), 15–17, 124–133, 136.

occur, however. Sometimes dying appears to be at least as terrible as the most fearful projections or imaginings of loving survivors.

But dying suddenly, by definition, does not take long; and consciousness ceases even sooner, ending the pain. Beyond the transition, there is an awakening to consciousness of the new living, in which the pain and suffering of the physical body are left behind. Those who lose a loved one to death, on the other hand, are left with myriads of questions. Many of those questions are cries of anguish more than they are queries to be answered—which is fortunate, because a worldview based on physical experience offers few answers that satisfy in such a moment. Even a limited realization that life continues after dying opens new ways of thinking about the loss, and awakens other emotions that eventually temper the grief.

Dying under care ～

Taking people of all ages into account, sudden death is less common than death after illness. Death from disease often occurs weeks or months—years in some cases—after first diagnosis. Older patients particularly may be under observation or treatment for two or more conditions, any one of which could have fatal consequences. When people have been living with such conditions for some time, dying comes as a combination of fulfilled expectation, shock, and relief.

Both my mother and my father died in this way. My mother's death at 57 came after more than a year confined to bed after exploratory surgery had revealed cancer in her liver (for which there was no medical treatment at all in the mid-1950s). Our family had become accustomed to her living in this way. The shadow of death had become so familiar that actual death came as a kind of shock, despite our long anticipation. A couple of decades later, my father was in his eighties when a series of small strokes and the onset of Parkinson's disease left him with a variety of physical and mental limitations and a sense that dying was imminent. In a very few weeks after moving from his room in a care facility to a room with full-time nursing care, he went into a coma and died in a few hours. Partly because of his more-advanced age and his expressed desire to get his dying over with, there was more relief and less shock than we had felt when my mother died.

Patients who die under these conditions are not necessarily better prepared for their transition to the new kind of living than those who die without warning. Hearing a diagnosis does not automatically change a person's thinking, intending, and acting—the only way in which knowledge can affect the spirit. Some people do take their physician's advice seriously enough to begin preparing themselves for living after dying, but in some ways it is more difficult to use knowledge of one's impending death for the shaping of character than it is to use other kinds of knowledge.

Emanuel Swedenborg's observations of souls discovering the deepest aspects of their identity show that changes of intention, and even of motive, have little effect on character formation when the changes are made under compulsion such as fear of dying or fear of punishment after death. This does not mean that people cannot continue forming or re-forming their life's pattern of values and purposes up until the moment of death. It does mean, however, that changes made because a person fears impending death may be little more than extensions of the deceit that had masked his or her true intentions all along. <u>On the other hand, people who take a diagnosis of some fatal disease as a significant reminder of the standing truth that they are going to die sometime, and use the reminder as an occasion to reevaluate and reorder their lives, can profit from the situation.</u>

This is a sobering idea, for all of us are in such a situation if we think of it. George Buttrick, one of the great preacher/scholars at Harvard University, told of being approached by a "dear, troubled, lady." Her husband had been diagnosed with untreatable cancer, and she was asking, "How can he stand it, Dr. Buttrick? How does he feel, knowing he is going to die?" "We know, don't we, dear lady?" Buttrick replied. "We're all dying . . . of mortality."

For those who approach—or look back on—the fuzzy and slippery boundary between middle age and old age, and watch their blood pressure and their weight rise relentlessly over years' visits to doctors, the issue becomes more pointed. Sherwin Nuland writes:

∽

Of hundreds of known diseases and their predisposing characteristics, some 85 percent of our aging population will succumb to the complications of only seven major entities: atherosclerosis, hypertension, adult-onset diabetes, obesity, mental depressing states such as Alzheimer's and other dementias, cancer, and decreased resistance to infection.[5]

∽

All who comprise that eighty-five percent group, or risk joining it, may look at death's transition as more than a the-

---

5. Nuland, 78.

oretical consideration. Since I am being treated for three of that "big seven," the creative process of writing recently about angels and now about dying has triggered some voluntary and involuntary introspection of my own values and purposes. The possibilities of self-deceit are as real for teachers as for learners. After all, our change-resisting nature is every bit as clever at evasive rationalizing as our change-seeking nature is at honest self-analysis. Having lived with these ideas for years adds greater responsibility. Making the best use of what there is to know about living after dying looks like an urgent task.

"Scheduled" dying ~

Among patients to whom or, more often, *of* whom a doctor has said their disease could be fatal, there are some whose prognosis includes a schedule for death. Enough patients and family members have pressed their doctor for a timetable, and enough physicians have offered one, that it has become commonplace for visitors to ask (out of the patient's hearing), "How long does he [or she] have left?"

Three problems, at least, are revealed by this cliché. One has to do with a physician's prediction that a patient's dying will take any specific number of months or weeks for completion. Anticipated schedules of this kind may have been more common when more diseases were considered untreatable and the course of a particular malady was reasonably consistent and predictable after the appearance of certain symptoms. The advent of many new treatments tends to make every illness a contest between nature and science (and often between spirit and science as well), in which scientists are reluctant to concede defeat. "Three months to live," "six weeks to live," or any schedules of that sort are misunderstood with amazing consistency by people trying to incorporate dying into the appointment book of their daily living. Both the patient's and the family's questions about the date of impending death and the physician's response are understandable, but different motives behind the asking and the answering lead to different interpretations of the information.

"Getting my affairs in order" is a time-worn formula that describes matters of surpassing importance to a person facing death. Patients who have the spiritual and psychological ability to handle the news and the mental and physical ability to take action feel a strong need to know the timetable implied in a fatal diagnosis. They have a lot to deal with. They have their own mortality to face in a specific way that may not have been possible before and certainly was avoidable until now. They have their own feelings about family, friends, and associates to consider, as well as the feelings those people have for them. They may have things regarding business or material assets or personal relationships they hope to accomplish in the time available to them—not simply the time remaining in their physical life, but the duration of their ability to do these things.

Families often have a need to gather from some distances for time with the patient while life and consciousness remain, and some kind of schedule may be significant to some members with conflicting responsibilities. In many cases, however, the request for a timetable reflects a desire for the comfort of stability and certainty in the face of an event that tends to destroy both for a while.

Doctors instinctively try to relieve suffering and even discomfort. Sensing one or both of these behind the question (particularly if it comes directly from the patient), they offer as much help as their training and experience can provide. Specialists have more experience with the particular disease but less knowledge of the particular patient, and tend to be more specific than generalists or family doctors in speaking of the time that death might occur. In any case, physicians are inclined by their scientific training to emphasize certain modifiers that are overlooked by patients or families seeking certainty. A prediction of "at least six months" may imply the possibility of a year or two; and "not more than a day or two" covers everything from half an hour to the next forty-eight. And even with the qualifiers, predictions are based on a generalized correlation between the patient's symptoms and statistical averages. Expecting precise accuracy in an individual case is like wading across a stream that averages twelve inches deep: it is easy to get in over one's head. "Grasping at straws" by converting the doctor's statistical probabilities into certainties, no matter how dearly desired, provides no real help to either the patient or attending loved ones.

Another problem with scheduled dying lies in the almost universal habit of speaking of mortality's timetables only where the patient cannot hear—or not hear clearly, which is worse. It must be obvious to everyone that *some* patients would be hurt more than they would be helped by being told certain details about their condition—a fatal prognosis, for example, or a timetable. However, this situation is not true as often as it seems obvious to loving family members who fear facing mortality and project even greater fear onto the person who is dying. Sometimes the "obvious need" for secrecy is a fear about sharing feelings, which is a fear of seizing an opportunity that all too soon will not be available.

In my mother's final illness, she was attended by a family

doctor who had known our whole family as patients for nearly twenty years. When he told the family about her cancer, the absence of any treatment, and the fatal prognosis, he also said that if she asked directly for a diagnosis he would tell her, but he would not force the information on her. He felt that if she were ready to handle it, she would ask; and if she didn't ask the question, she wasn't ready to hear the answer.

The doctor knew my mother fairly well: in fact, she first asked my wife, in a private moment, and my wife followed our doctor's plan. On a later visit by the doctor, when my mother felt ready to share the issue with all of us at once, she asked him. There were tears at the time, but no regrets later.

Just over two decades later, when my father was dying, our common knowledge was shared less well. I described him earlier as wanting to die. It would be more accurate to say that he looked forward to death, but feared a painful death. Having talked once about this with him, we spoke no more about the process.

As he approached death, he grew increasingly numb (unlike the months of agony he had witnessed in his wife and feared now for himself). After he entered the final coma, we had a family farewell at his bedside: our daughters, my wife, and I holding hands in a circle that included his hands. We prayed together, repeating the twenty-third psalm, giving thanks for our life with him and asking for a peaceful death when it was time. We said goodbye and told him it was all right to die now; and my wife and I both felt (or believe we felt) a slight squeeze from his hand in response. A few minutes later, while I was sitting beside his bed, he coughed gently and died. There are reliable accounts of people hearing and remembering what was said when they were in a coma or unconscious from sedation, so I have at least the comfort of a theoretical possibility that Dad and I shared that last exchange.

These experiences, those of friends, and numerous others who have written about death make a quite convincing case: except in the most unusual circumstances, the pain involved in sharing knowledge of impending death is less than the pain of patient and loved ones keeping such a vital secret from each other.

Scheduled dying often raises another issue, namely, the assumption that the patient's death will bring an end to everything. If there is debate, it centers on the truth of the claim that living continues after dying. The absence of certain proof on either side leaves little ground for rational debate but does not stop the argument. Nevertheless, the question "How much time does he have left?" implies an attitude that is even less helpful than the refusal to discuss death with one who is dying. The two issues seem related: why be so protective of hope as to lie to a dying person, and at the same time refuse to share the hope that living will continue after the physical body has died?

This is not meant to imply that belief in continuing life is going to wipe away all of a dying person's problems. The terrible immediacy of pain is not always diminished by a promise of pie-in-the-sky-bye-and-bye, even a promise that can be fulfilled. The impending loss of so much that has been important in physical life is not denied by even the surest hope of another way of living. My mother had no doubt about the continuing nature of living; but in the moment our family shared with her the knowledge of her dying, she claimed her chief grief to be that "I won't get to see the girls grow up" (speaking of my daughters, then two and four).

At the end of "The Great Lover," his love song to animate and inanimate physical beauty, Rupert Brooke wrote of the losses facing everyone in whom the ties that have held spiritual and physical realities together are about to be dissolved:

∾

Oh, never a doubt but, somewhere, I shall wake,
And give what's left of love again, and make
New friends, now strangers. . . .
                    But the best I've known
Stays here, and changes, breaks, grows old, is blown
About the winds of the world, and fades from brains
Of living men, and dies.
                    Nothing remains.

∾

Certainty of waking somewhere in a spiritual world promises new joys but does not prevent loss of much that is familiar, much that is dear. While the human spirit retains everything of eternal value in the new way of living beyond dying, nothing does remain of the physical aspects of things, and these have been important in our lives. Added to those perceived losses, the dying person shares the grief that radiates from the faces of loved ones gathered around. Dying can be painful to the body and the spirit, with or without hope for living after dying.

Recognizing the pain, the loss, the grief of dying, it remains true that all of these things are experienced in a context. It may be, for some, that enduring all these hardships simply to reach the end of living becomes a hardship in itself. But there is another perspective. Enduring the same trials as a difficult transition to something new and fulfilling puts them in the context of other changes and transitions that are remembered as having been tough-to-get-through ordeals that, once survived, fade in comparison to the greater and more lasting experiences that followed. Men remember the teenaged agony of asking the most beautiful girl in school for a date, just as, in a different order of reality, mothers remember childbirth: some of our most joyous memories were the outgrowth of our most difficult trials. Knowing that there is an end beyond dying, a change foreseen in the not-too-distant future, can transform the experience of dying from hardship to expectation, from sorrow to joy. Those who cannot foster that hope at least ought not to dampen it.

Physical failing ∾

Catastrophic dying, dying under care, and scheduled dying differ from each other far less than they are alike. All are sequences of physical failing as the body loses its ability to support the compound life of a spirit enveloped in a body. The organs and systems of the human body are so intricately and intimately interrelated that it is rare for one organ's failure to cause death without involving others (if, in fact, that is possible at all). Partial or total failure of one system or organ causes stress and failure in others. The organ in which the initial failure occurred may, or may not, appear on the death certificate as the cause of the person's dying.

In healthy young adults receiving massive, fatal trauma in an accident, the sequence of failures is rapid enough to appear simultaneous; but the part of the body that is injured or destroyed actually starts a high-speed chain reaction. Consciousness may cease instantaneously, but death involves cessation of activity of the heart, lungs, and brain. Although all these stop working soon after any one fails, there are few accidents that stop them all at once.

In people under attack from a chronic disease, the primary disease affects the entire body, directly or indirectly putting stress on other systems. Sometimes the stress is so debilitating that death's immediate cause may be the failure of an organ that was normal at the time the original diagnosis was made. People of more advanced age are apt to find that two or more systems or organs are weakened enough to pose a threat to life if left untreated—whether treatment consists of surgery, medication, or changes in personal lifestyle. In a longer term, all of these failing systems threaten life even if they are treated. Any one of them, or a related system stressed by them, can fail to such an extent that treatment cannot prevent collapse of the whole vital system.

Sherwin Nuland develops this point in *How We Die*, Nuland argues that people *do* die of old age. They die simply because their body can no longer sustain life, despite the universal practice of naming the final failure of a system or organ as the "cause of death" on death certificates. He also encourages an attitude that avoids disruptive or "heroic" measures to treat a failing organ or system when a number of others are lined up, as it were, to cause the patient's death if the first one is prevented from doing so.

I can add the accounts of my mother's and my father's dying to the argument in favor of allowing the body to fail and die when it obviously is ready to do that. My mother's doctor had warned us of the probability of pneumonia, suggesting that he would not treat it with antibiotics unless we really wanted him to do so. We agreed and felt relieved at the brevity of her final decline when it came (even though we, especially my father, were somewhat shocked by its suddenness). In my father's latter days, I had asked his physician (who had not known him long) about the likelihood of pneumonia, and we agreed to follow the same policy as we had with my mother. I happened to be out of town when he fell into a coma, and I flew back to find him comatose, breathing with a very loud and raspy sound. I telephoned the doctor to ask for an oxygen tent to ease his breathing. Instead of ordering one, the doctor reminded me of our agreement not to treat the pneumonia. "Not try to cure it," I responded, "but to keep him comfortable." "Is he conscious," the doctor asked? "No," I answered. "Then whom do you want the oxygen *for?*"

We left Dad as he was and formed the prayer circle, already described, that preceded his death. I still believe that the doctor—and my earlier decision—was right. There was no medical justification for doing anything under those circumstances. Dad was ready, and his body was ready, for the transition to another kind of living. My discomfort at the sound of his breathing was not a valid excuse for forcibly prolonging the body/spirit union after the time for its separation had come.

The choice is not always so clear or so easy to make from a human perspective. It can be hard to distinguish between treatment that brings comfort and treatment that only forces unnecessary prolongation of physical life and its concomitant pain. When the difference can be discerned, however, the course that allows completion of the transition already in progress is the course of wisdom and of love.

A decision to withhold treatment, or to implement an earlier decision to do so, most often is made after the patient is unconscious. For a loved one at the bedside, the possibility of communication through the barrier of a coma offers the only means of accomplishing something that seems most urgent. One of these is giving the patient permission to die. Many people in such a situation intuit an effort by the patient to hang on for the sake of those who love him or her, wanting to free them of this burden. Within that intuition, or closely tied to it, is a desire to accomplish a crucial bit of grief work. Saying something like "I want to see you get well, but if you need to die now, it is all right with me" serves both purposes. It may help a lot to add, "I'll be okay," reminding the patient and yourself that the grief of loss will pass. The difficulty of forcing the words out is a sign of their significance for the latter purpose. Repeating them, at intervals during the vigil, may increase the possibility of finding the patient at a receptive moment and certainly reinforces the effect on the speaker.

There is another pattern of physical failing that imposes a different set of challenges on both patient and loving supporters. Alzheimer's disease is the best known of various dementias that attack the elderly and—either with increasing frequency of occurrence or increasing frequency of diagnosis—people in late-middle-age, or even younger. When memory has been destroyed and with it the recognition of friends and loved ones, and even personal identity, the person who is remembered and loved seems absent from the form that still needs care. Spouses, siblings, or children, caring for a patient with or without the help of hospice or nursing homes, have good reason to wonder what meaning, purpose, or value can be found in the patient's continued living. Body and spirit appear connected; but with the recognizable and recognizing mind apparently absent, the point of the connection becomes unclear. Long after the patient has lost the ability to anticipate any future event, people around him or her are left with no prospects more desirable than losing their loved one to death. Death is kinder than these diseases that take away the loved one and leave only a breathing image to care for and weep over.

The sequence of physical failing that precedes dying may be predictable and peaceful, as when people die quietly in old age; it may be sudden and frightening to experience or to watch; it may be unpredictable and frustrating. We have no more control over this prelude to dying than we have over the manner of dying itself. But we can control, at least in part, our preparation for it, in the life we are living now. That preparation affects, even transforms, our attitude toward dying.

Being there ~

One need not nearly die to experience the nearness of death. Patients come close to death in many ways other than cardiopulmonary arrest, which sometimes occasions the dramatic and much-discussed psychic events that Raymond Moody, Kenneth Ring, and others have called "near-death experiences" or "NDEs." More often, however, people change from apparently healthy to "critical" (meaning that death is an imminent possibility) in a few hours or days, or progress from a chronic condition to a critical state in a similar length of time. This is also a kind of near-death experience, although the patient does not see a "tunnel" or "bright light" and doesn't as often report seeing an angel.

The approach toward death in such circumstances must be considered an experience of those at the bedside—loved ones or supporting friends—as well as of the patient (who often is comatose or barely conscious as a consequence of the illness or of medication for it). It is an experience for which the spectacular advances of modern medical science offer little aid. Psychological counselors skilled in guiding people through such difficulties seldom are at the right place at the right time (except for hospice workers and some hospital chaplains who have the training and a special concern for such issues). Whatever guidance or support may be offered, however, the pain is intensely personal.

Part of the pain is a combination of separation-anxiety and loneliness, a loneliness that may be shared but not ameliorated by the presence of other loved ones at the bedside. One avenue of relief is doing something with the patient. Grooming, reading aloud, reporting on friends' activities, reminiscing, helping with a meal, bathing, listening to music, or writing letters for the patient, all may be somewhat satisfying forms of such activities.

A much deeper and more gratifying common activity is an exercise in deep breathing coordinated between the attendant and the patient. Sometimes called "cross breathing," especially by those familiar with the traditions of *The Tibetan Book of the Dead*, it can induce comfort and even peace in patient and attendant alike. Coordinated by directions from the attendant for as long as necessary, the exercise consists of slow, deep breathing—a deep breath in, holding it, exhaling concerns and tensions along with the breath—then pausing, breathing in, holding, and out again—repeating for as long as you can concentrate on your breathing to the exclusion of other thoughts.

When the coordination has been practiced enough that it can continue spontaneously, the out-breath can be softly vocalized. A natural "ahhh" will do, although a sound bearing serious or sacred significance may likely be better. Following Tibetan traditions, the universal sacred sound "ohmmm" may be used; or, from the Christian tradition,

Kyrie Jesu, "Lord Jesus," or a similar phrase. With practice, this can be continued for fifteen or twenty minutes. The patient may fall asleep during the exercise, and the sleep is likely to be quieter and more restful than before. A patient already near death may die peacefully.

The experience of staying with a patient who is dying (or might be dying, within the range of diagnostic ambiguity) is difficult in unexpected ways. Most of us develop familiar ways of coping with crises. Whether we take pride in our crisis management or deplore it, we recognize it as familiar and fairly predictable. Few of us have as much practice at dealing with a *potentially* immanent crisis. Attending someone who nears death without either entering it or moving away from it is painful, and disturbingly unclear. What to hope for—physical life or physical death—becomes as unclear as what to expect. Hospitals or sub-acute care facilities are awkward, as well as cheerless, places to wait; and the wait near death can last for hours, for days, even for weeks. Where hospice is available, and the patient qualifies, many (if not most) of these concerns can be alleviated to a significant degree. It is an option that should be explored with the charge nurse, supervisor, and attending physician.

Whatever professionals can do, waiting involves many hours alone with the patient. Almost imperceptibly, the circumstances of such a vigil induce a kind of "tunnel vision," in which the patient's prognosis and the attender's prospective loss become the watcher's whole universe. The friend, counselor, or therapist, any of whom might help to expand the attendant's horizons, probably is not there at the crucial moment. Extended waiting also affects life outside the hospital, where job, family, and the world proceed without regard for the seeming suspension of time and emotion in the sickroom. Outside tasks and responsibilities that can be postponed are postponed, until they become crises, competing with the patient for attention.

Almost the only help available is from spiritual sources. That help might come in the form of a fragment of a thought that seems irrelevant, but actually is more to-the-point than we realize. I recall one bedside moment of deep depression, when I suddenly was reminded of the mealtime grace my family said: "O, give thanks unto the Lord, for he is good; for his mercy is forever" (Psalm 107). I started to dismiss the thought as an intrusion (giving thanks is most disruptive to self-pity!), but I blocked the impulse. Immediately then, my mind was flooded with memories of the life I had had with this woman I loved, and I realized how much I had to be thankful for.

Since it is common for patients to reach a stage where death would be imminent if medical means of maintaining heart and lung functions were not available, attendants face another problem. Decisions between death and artificial life support can be helped enormously by careful discussion before the need arises and by counseling at the time. But such decisions are heart-wrenching in any case. They may have to be made without warning after certain accidents or internal incidents, in the brief and highly stressed moments when resuscitation must be begun if biological life is to be preserved, or withheld if it is to be ended. On the other hand, the question of a body's living or dying may loom as a choice that might have to be made at some early or distant point in the waiting process, in the event that what feels like a struggle between life and death reaches an apparent stalemate in which continued biological function may or may not be deemed living.

A possible complication to this already difficult situation may be handled more easily by being prepared for it. If the family, or lone loving attendant, decides with the physician to withhold further treatment and allow the patient to die, it remains possible for the patient to revive spontaneously and begin to improve. When this happens, the loved one at the bedside may unexpectedly feel troubled, and even fall prone to guilt over being upset that the patient is getting better. Such unanticipated reversals in the outcome of life's decisions can be seriously traumatic to already tortured emotions. Employing another imperfect metaphor, the psychic rollercoaster ride from fear of loss, to resignation to loss, to uncertain hope can produce a variety of unexpected emotions. Advance awareness of the possibility may help avoid feelings of guilt.

Not every patient lingers long in this uncertain vestibule to death, nor forces such decisions on attending families or friends. It seems irrelevant to ask whether those who have such bedside near-death experiences are more or less fortunate than those who lose a loved one suddenly to a massive heart attack or catastrophic highway accident, or watch and wait through a long, painful, and apparently inevitable decline due to cancer or AIDS. Stress, grief, denial, anger, and illusions of solitude and unique affliction—all accompany the loss of those we have loved, however that loss occurs. Whatever we feel, the same spiritual guidance and support are available to survivors in all conditions.

Expectations ∿

Earlier, I referred to Sherwin Nuland's *How We Die*. If the discussion of death scenes here has any special interest for you, I cannot recommend too strongly Nuland's excellent book. His starting point is, indeed, different from mine: as a scientist, he is as resolutely skeptical of the possibility of "a blissful afterlife,"[6] as I, a theologian, am confident that living continues beyond dying. But I solidly support his recommendations.

One theme that Nuland explores in several contexts needs to be emphasized here. He tells of many patients, and patients' companions, who had hoped for a dignity, a stillness, a beauty in dying that simply was not to be experienced. Instead they found dying bitter and ugly. Typically, it was hidden from loving family or friends behind swinging doors or hastily drawn curtains, and it was attended by strangers, machines, confusion, and pain. Nuland has found "death with dignity" to be a tragically unrealistic hope for the majority of people.

One of the antidotes Nuland recommends for the undignified tradition of hospital deaths and other faults of the modern way of dying is a return to an emphasis on family practice in medicine. Family doctors know their patients better than specialists do (specialists seldom having seen their patients before being called in during the late stages of an illness) and are less likely to call for dramatic intervention in a dying process that might be prolonged but not forestalled. Under this kind of care, more patients would die at home or a hospital room (rather than a hospital operating room or intensive-care unit). While dignified dying is not guaranteed under such conditions, it is possible in more cases than under the present system in most communities. Not enough doctors practice family medicine these days to make the more-humane care they can provide available to everyone, although hospice can help in many cases. Nuland's recommendation can guide many patients toward a better chance for a better death.

---

6. Nuland, 138.

During the last stages of her physical life, my wife came under the care of a physician in family practice who specialized in care for the dying. Although he had not known Marian as a vital and active person, the doctor appeared to recognize the remnants of those qualities and treated her with a respect that probably was as evident to her as it was to me. He was willing to discontinue medications that did not make her feel better, to prescribe pain-relievers without fear of her becoming addicted, and to call for hospice services when death became imminent. His concern for what was important to his patient, coupled with Marian's acceptance of what was happening, endowed her dying process with a dignity that I felt at the time but did not identify by name until rereading Nuland.

Emanuel Swedenborg, looking at death from the far side of the transition, offered a description of an ideal way of dying that would be possible in a more nearly ideal physical and spiritual environment. In that situation, he says,

∽

people would be free of disease. There would be only a decline in extreme old age, when they became children again, but wise children. And then when the body could no longer serve the inner person, the spirit, people would cross without illness from their earthly bodies into the kind of bodies angels have straight from this world into heaven.

Arcana Coelestia 5726

∽

We may draw from this the image of a sequence of declining functions in the body's organs and systems, so that strength and mobility would be reduced gradually until the whole vital system finally shut down. The end would be essentially painless, even voluntary to some degree, as we decide when to fall asleep at the end of the day.

The internal and external conditions for this kind of dying are not available to most of us in our time. We must expect one or another of the types of death that Nuland describes—some of which are closer to Swedenborg's ideal than others. Our attitude toward dying can affect the manner of our dying to some extent (greater or lesser, depending on the disease that precipitates our death), and approaching death as a transition between different kinds of living is the most helpful approach available.

11 ～

Supporting Characters

[T]he theatrical imagery, from which "Death Scenes" was drawn as a title for the preceding chapter, also provides a title (and its interpretation) for this one. Of course, some people die without relatives or even friends, so not all death scenes have supporting characters in this sense, although there may be some unseen by medical professionals. The angels and spirits who gather around dying humans to make their transition as easy as it can be also might be called supporting characters. The two sets of characters need to be distinguished, however: this chapter is about physical people, and the next will be about spirits.

Close family ～

For many of us, the ideal image of "death with dignity," or "a good death," includes the patient's family gathered around the deathbed. Each member of the circle would have a chance to express his or her love and say goodbye. As noted previously, this ideal is realized only as a rare privilege, granted at random, so far as we know, to very few. On the other hand, not all deaths are totally bereft of dignity. People do die under circumstances that differ from the ideal in varying degrees, loved ones do offer support in late stages of dying, and they do receive responses from, and feel a sense of closure with, the person who dies. Circumstances seldom permit these things to be as good—as supportive, unambiguous, and satisfying—as we would like; but they are not always completely absent, either. In dying, as in living, we have to make do with the best we can get.

A friend whom I'll call "Helen" lost her aging mother, "Norma," after a series of diagnostic and palliative medical procedures, none of which provided any clear prognosis or long-lasting improvement. For several months, Helen had lived in her mother's house to care for her, visiting her own home only occasionally to get clothes or some other necessities. The time they had together in this arrangement was marred for both of them by bickering that arose out of the mother's denial of her illnesses and resistance to being confined and cared for.

A little over a week before her actual death, Norma collapsed one evening, apparently dying. She lost consciousness; but, after a few minutes, she revived again after what seemed to Helen to have been a near-death event—although her mother did not speak of any "experience" during the episode. Helen wondered what pulled her mother back to the unhappy, uncertain life she was living.

A few days after this event, Helen received a totally unexpected surprise. She had two sisters in distant cities and a brother from whom none of the family had heard in thirty years. A neighbor of her mother's, who had known of the lost son and Norma's impending death, knocked at the door one evening to say she had instigated a search and located the brother: Helen should expect a call from him later that night! He did call and agreed to attend a reunion at Norma's home of all four siblings with their mother in a few days. He and the two out-of-town sisters spoke with their mother by telephone. The reunion took place as scheduled but brought only the siblings together. Norma died in the same manner that she had almost died a few days before while she and Helen were preparing for the brother's arrival.

Her death illustrates several of the ways in which dying can differ from the ideal without abandoning it altogether. For Helen, the event had many attributes of the ideal. After upsetting confrontations with several doctors, with nurses in a series of hospitals, and even with hospice personnel, her mother died quietly, at home, with her daughter by her side. As close as it came to being a "good death," however, the event felt to my friend distinctly short of the ideal. New and former doctors had been recommending different courses of treatment, divergence of purposes had been forcing a separation from hospice care. Up to just before the end, Helen and Norma were struggling with unanswerable questions about choices between "comforting" and "disease-prolonging" courses of action. The siblings were coming, but they had not arrived. The death was sudden, expected-but-unexpected, and upsetting.

For Helen's brother and sisters, it seemed much farther from the ideal. They had not been with Norma when she died, or even in the last months of her life; the brother had not seen his mother for more than thirty years. Still, all of them had spoken to her a day or so before her death, and they knew that she died knowing her son was coming home. When they got together, old resentments proved to have been outlived; they began to enjoy one another's company, found no serious disagreements over dividing their mother's property, and made plans to see more of one another. They talked of being grateful to their mother for bringing them together, even if it was by dying that she did it. Helen felt certain that, all in all, it could have been much worse.

Surviving family members are not the only ones who suffer when dying differs from the ideal. As with Norma's family, physical distances and psychic distances (such as those involved with the decades of no communication) present serious obstacles. Relationships between patient and family, even when close, sometimes are a kind of "close combat" that renders tender farewells or a last-minute change of heart unnatural, if even possible. Not infrequently, a family's difficulty in facing death and loss raises barriers of denial and secrecy that add to the dying patient's discomfort and suffering.

With all of these potential personal roadblocks added to the barricades set up by doctors and hospitals for reasons of sanitation, convenience, protection against lawsuits, or pure corporate insensitivity, it may seem remarkable that dying ever is a time of peace for the patient and of healing for the bereaved. Nevertheless, it can be all of that. Sometimes it is.

I had two aunts, my father's sisters, who lived together in their latter years and died a couple of years apart. Their stories illustrate a few of the aspects of dying that allow it to be as good as it occasionally is, despite the obstacles.

My older aunt, "Alice," was my father's twin. When she entered a nursing home with senile dementia, we postponed telling Dad (in retrospect, perhaps unwisely) because of a fear of depressing him. It was on my next visit with him, however, that he began speaking of his fear of dying painfully and of wishing it (the dying) were over. He died soon enough after this conversation that the phrase "he willed himself dead" seems a plausible description of what happened. My other aunt, "June," decided not to tell Aunt

Alice that her twin brother had died. It was some months later that my wife and I visited the two aunts across the country from our home, and June asked if I would break the news of my father's death to his twin. We were not sure when, if ever, Alice understood what was being said to her: her expression seldom changed, and it was still more rare for her to speak intelligible words. But when I told her that Dad had died, she looked up at me, nodded solemnly, and clearly said, "I know."

This account is not clear evidence of psychic communication between fraternal twins. But the two episodes— Dad's concern with his own mortality coming immediately after his sister was institutionalized, no one having told him about it; and Alice's knowledge of Dad's death when no one had told her—at least raise the possibility that people approaching the transition to purely spiritual living may become open to spiritual ways of knowing.

Sometimes this enables dying people to know things their bedside companions cannot share or may misunderstand, especially at first hearing. My wife's mother, during the months before she died of Alzheimer's disease, often spoke of how "we've decided not to stay here; we'll be going home before long," and of being "ready to go home." She was in the infirmary of the retirement center where she had moved with Marian's father, so he usually corrected her with a reminder that they *were* home. Once, she answered such a correction with, "No, my mother is getting things ready for me to come home." "But your mother's dead," he responded; and she looked at him with a patient curiosity suggesting that she had become accustomed to people's saying senseless things like that. I am convinced now that she really had seen her mother with her spiritual eyes and that, in an inarticulate way, she knew that her body would soon release her and she could "go home."

Alice died a few months after the visit in which I told her of Dad's death; and in less than a year after that, June suffered a small stroke and broke her hip when she fell. She acquired limited mobility with a walker, but mostly was confined to bed for the months before her death. Habitually a cheerful and outgoing person, she appeared so happy to see every relative, friend, and professional who came into her room that more than one visitor remarked on *her* brightening *their* day when they had come to cheer her up. She gave no indication of pain or concern about the bed sores that developed, and gave many signs of continuing and pervasive happiness.

My daughter had married and moved to the city where June lived and visited her occasionally; but, after June's fall and confinement, she visited her great-aunt every day. Toward the end, when June seemed drowsy, or slipping in and out of a coma, my daughter would read to her from the Bible. One day, she was finishing the last chapter of the book of Revelation. As she read, "Behold, I come quickly" (22:7), she heard movement in the bed. Looking up, she saw June smiling and trying to raise her head, then collapsing on the pillow with a peaceful, still expression. After a few moments she realized that June was no longer breathing. Whatever she had or had not heard of what was read to her in the coma, for whatever reason, she smiled and tried to rise up, and collapsed, no longer breathing. June died in apparent peace.

The value to a dying person of having a loved one or a friend present may not always be obvious to a grieving attendant, who feels cut off from the patient by coma, impediments to speech, or mental dysfunction. But my experience with my family reinforces what I have heard and read from many sources, namely, that a loved one's voice, touch, or scent—what I can only call an "aura of presence"—is perceived by patients who cannot acknowledge them or respond in any way; and that these perceptions are deeply comforting and reassuring. To this must be added what the loving companion knows, perhaps without realizing it consciously or even accepting it at that moment: the experience comforts, sustains, and enhances the life of the one who watches, grieves, and cares.

Close friends ∾

There are many cases in which a blurred distinction, if any, separates family from close friends. In some of these, if the distinction is made, the friends are closer than the family. This happens in many instances of a rift of some kind within the family, perhaps most typically today involving sexual preference and/or AIDS; but it comes about, too, where the family is normally close, but an extraordinary relationship makes a friend even closer.

Friends, however close, often are at a disadvantage, compared to relatives, when a friend is dying in a hospital. Hospital rules regarding visitors, especially visits to seriously ill or terminal patients, vary widely. No matter where hospital regulations draw the line that excludes all but a very few visitors, friends usually are excluded. Sometimes, when there are no family members visiting, friends are allowed; but it is an exception, usually brought about by a persuasive individual who can plead or argue to gain admission to the bedside. The need to justify a visit to one's closest friend seems an unfair burden at a difficult time to many a grieving friend. Perhaps it is a (rare) beneficial by-product of the

AIDS epidemic, but there is growing evidence that friends with various relationships to patients are getting more respect at some hospitals.

On the other hand, friends frequently have an advantage, compared to relatives, in the level of openness and intimacy that is acceptable in bedside conversation. Family members tend to bring a lot of historical baggage into the sickroom—baggage accumulated when parents kept (or thought they kept) secrets from children, and children didn't reveal their adolescent emotions to parents. These unspoken rules of silence can prevent people from saying what they most urgently need to say (and most urgently need to hear). Probably there is little that can be done about such barriers when they have stood unchallenged until the time of a death-vigil; but the tragic solitude that they impose on people—physically close enough to be holding hands—can be envisioned before that time, and something can be done about them in less stressful circumstances.

The comfort of friends in a moment of crisis can be seen from how often a sick person may refer to a childhood friend, long dead perhaps, or an old acquaintance. An incident during our last visit with Aunt Alice, accompanied by Aunt June, is also intriguing. My wife mentioned to Alice that her room was bright and cheerful, with a courtyard outside the window. Alice looked out, smiled, and said several words. We understood only "flowers" and, a little later, "people walking." The courtyard was, to our eyes (I almost wrote, "was in fact"), a parched bit of desert enclosed by wings of the nursing home, with one small tree that may have had leaves at one time standing in the center. June started to correct Alice, but my wife intervened and asked if she recognized anyone who was walking in the garden. "Yes, there's Frank, and . . . , " she began, before the expressionless mask and the confused mumbling of her dementia took over again. "Frank," I remembered, was one of the people who gathered every week at Alice's house to play bridge when I was a boy.

An old woman whom I viewed as sweet but flaky in my self-confident years of young fatherhood used to speak of talking things over with her dead husband every night before going to sleep. I regarded her at that time as walking only very lightly on the same earth I did. But in retrospect I realize that, until she was well into her eighties, she maintained a busy round of corresponding and visiting that really helped a circle of her sick and house-bound friends; and I sense she got a lot of help with the emotional strain of dealing with the elderly and the dying by talking out her problems every night with her husband's spirit.

The divinely protected freedom of choice, discussed in the chapter "Continuing Identity" keeps people who are not already convinced of the reality of continuing life from recognizing the source of their support as clearly as my "flaky" friend did; but hidden clues reveal comforting spiritual presences with people who need them. When a friend of Aunt Alice was dying of cancer, she spoke often of her friend who had shared a home with her for many years, showing (to my understanding) that the friend was with her in mind and spirit during those difficult days. And a friend of mine dreamed often of his childhood buddy during the weeks before he died, suggesting a similar relationship.

Attending professionals ⌁

In modern hospital practice, a large number and wide variety of medical personnel are involved with every patient.

Frequently they become involved with the patient's family and friends as well. One dimension of the variety is the hierarchy of hospital staffs. There may be orderlies, aides, candy-stripers, nursing technicians, LPNs, RNs, nursing supervisors, specialty nurses, specialty nursing supervisors, interns, staff physicians, attending physicians, specialist's assistants, specialists, and many more—most of them changing faces three times a day. In a teaching hospital, with its additional hierarchy of students and its tradition of rounds in which patients becomes case studies, the list of bedside attendants grows even longer. Each of these people, except the patient and visitors, knows the chain of command-and-responsibility (the pecking order) in which all function. The bigger the hospital is, the better the chances are of finding the special treatment most perfectly suited to the patient's individual malady. However, the bigger the hospital is, the harder it is to discover the right person to ask for what the patient needs at any given time.

Fortunately or otherwise, this choice of a hospital with its double edge of greater expertise verses greater complexity is one few of us ever make for ourselves. If we have a family physician or a primary-care physician in a larger clinic, we probably will visit the specialists we are told to see and enter the hospital chosen by our primary or specializing physician. Still, patients and patients' family and friends could be far better prepared than most of us find ourselves to encounter the legions of medical professionals with whom we will deal.

Professionals who know the hospital routine can be helpful before you enter a hospital. Preparation far in advance may seem of little value because of all the changes that may occur before the need arises. When such preparations are made, however, they prove more helpful than expected in many cases. When you approach or reach retirement age, you ought to talk to your primary physician about possible future hospitalization and the choices available. Visit the hospital (or hospitals), talk to administrative or admitting personnel (the first receptionist inside the door will direct you to the right place), and learn what you can about what to expect. Ask particularly about documents you may be asked to read and sign. After all, the information gained in a preliminary visit, free from immediate anxiety, will be much more usable than when you enter as a sick patient, perhaps being carried from an ambulance into the emergency room.

For several years, I received medical care from a primary physician and several specialists in a large clinic with hundreds of physicians and an attached hospital. After visiting many times for a variety of reasons, I felt quite at home in the place (although I remember thinking, after being sent to a series of specialists for a round of tests, that I now knew how a pinball must feel). But one winter day, after nursing a self-diagnosed case of the flu for a couple days before a three-day-and-night journey home in an AMTRAK pullman compartment, I entered the clinic's emergency room with a temperature of 108 and pneumonia in both lungs. In that condition, I felt totally overwhelmed by two documents that were handed me, each consisting of several pages of single-spaced type and somewhat legalistic language. One document listed my rights as a patient entering the hospital, and the other was concerned with directives to be followed in case certain treatment options should arise in the course of my disease. I was given all the time I wanted to study them, but I remember thinking that what I really needed was time to study them before I got so sick. After looking blankly at them for several minutes, I signed on the dotted lines, committing perjury by my affirmation that I had "carefully read and understood" both documents.

This experience taught me I should get samples of the documents that will be offered me in my next hospitalization and read them while I am healthy. There is another group of documents that call for careful and deliberate consideration before one arrives at a hospital admitting office or emergency room. In my state, they are called the Medical Power of Attorney (MPO), Advance Directives (AD), and Do Not Resuscitate (DNR) order. The feeling of unique difficulty that pervades arriving at a hospital as a patient, or accompanying one, tends to be diluted when questions about an MPO, AD, and DNR make it obvious that the "unique" problems are dealt with in preprinted forms with standardized acronyms. However routine the decisions may seem to emergency-room nurses, the life-and-death decisions are heart-wrenching in the distress and grief of the moment. Indeed, it is a relief to the medical staff, as well as to the patient or caretaker, if copies of signed, notarized documents of this kind have been signed before check-in. Doctors, lawyers, social workers, and others, individually or as a team, can help you work through the options and the process of decision-making.

When a patient enters the phase I have called "scheduled dying," and the prognosis is for less than a year, both the patient and the loving attender may receive extremely valuable help from a hospice organization. If the attending physician, head nurse, or social worker does not suggest hospice care, it is important that the patient or caregiver ask one or all of them about it. Eligibility and specific arrangements may vary from city to city and from case to case; but when hospice care is available, it should be pursued. There are arrangements for home care, care in special hospice institutions, and for hospice nurses, technicians, and social workers to provide an added layer of care in nursing homes and assisted living situations. These people, with their special training and experience in caring for the dying, offer unique, comforting, invaluable assistance.

Unfortunately, not all professionals will be helpful to you. Medical and religious professionals, for instance, are busy in hospital rooms often enough that they occasionally encounter each other there. The overwhelming majority of people in the helping professions are truly committed to their patients, and welcome all the help they can get from any source with the same goal. However, there are a few whose attitudes toward other professionals are unpredictable. There are surgeons who suspect internists of being potential opponents at some critical stage of the patient's treatment, specialists who scorn family doctors, older physicians who are suspicious of younger ones, nurses who disagree with doctors on a prescribed medication, and so on. Of course, some people do not trust anyone other than themselves whether they are dealing with doctors, ministers, lawyers, insurance investigators, or lay people innocently standing around. But the line between some doctors (from any specialty) and religious professionals—priests, ministers, rabbis, deacons—seems especially provocative in a hospital setting.

Experience tends to toughen the hide of professionals against the subtle or not-so-subtle antagonism of other professionals; but few patients or sick-room visitors are so unfortunate as to be experienced at this kind of unprofessional behavior among those on whom they depend so completely. There is little if anything that lay people can do about crossfire of this kind, unless they have the sort of aggressive personality that allows them, in the midst of their own personal crisis, to point out to the professionals just what they see going on. Short of that kind of confrontation, a patient's or visitor's best defense is an understanding that this kind of thing does happen, even in and between the most prestigious of professions, and that few professionals will be seriously diverted from their most effective care for the patient by interplay of this kind.

At times, of course, the divergent perspectives of different specialists may have a beneficial effect—as in dialectic logic, the opposition of a thesis and an antithesis produces a synthesis. An internist and a surgeon, each arguing for a different course of treatment, may inspire one or the other (or a third party in the consultation) to think of a third alternative that is more promising than either of the first two. On the other hand, medical/clerical arguments, or intrareligious ones, seldom are helpful to the patient or the visitors: they are best confined to other venues—the classroom, the professional association meeting, even the hallway (well away from the patient's room). However, I have watched uncomfortably when they were not.

Awareness of these problems has surfaced in professional journals and workshops, so distressing illustrations may well become scarcer with time. For now, unfortunate patient/victims have allies. The family doctor who referred you to the specialist whose attitude proves troubling, your pastor or the hospital chaplain (whichever was not involved in the confrontation), a social worker or milieu therapist connected to your case, even a hospital or community ombudsman—any of these can be enlisted for the minimal intervention that should be necessary. After all, most people work in the helping professions because they really want to help, and a discreet reminder usually is sufficient when irrelevant factors have led them to present unhelpful or disturbing appearances.

The funeral ∽

From one perspective, there is truth in a saying I once heard from a Japanese student: we are born alone and we die alone. There is another, more obvious viewpoint from which virtually no one dies alone. People who die unexpectedly, when no one else is in the room or the house, still leave family or associates with a variety of rituals to complete. People who are homeless or have no next of kin still die within the structures of society, and leave someone—usually a government functionary—to perform these rituals, however routinely and dispassionately. Only the hypothetical "man on a desert island" can die "alone" in the sense of dying without affecting anyone, leaving no one with obligatory rituals connected with his dying. Whoever inherits responsibility for these rituals turns to another set of professionals—morticians or funeral directors.

Jessica Mitford's classic study *The American Way of Death* (1963) may overstate the case against American funeral practices and practitioners; but a moderate and evenhanded book would not have sold nearly as well. There are many funeral directors who have made a personal commitment to conduct their business as a helping profession and have eased the difficulty of survivors' rituals for many people. On the other hand, Mitford is even more likely to understate the case against American funeral homes and their sales practices. There are few consumers more vulnerable to sales pressure than loving survivors, and few markets have developed sales techniques that make greater use of the powerful emotions of guilt, sorrow, and loyalty than are practiced in the funeral business.

The clergy, too, has an interest in helping people who have survived the death of a loved one. This interest is so opposed to the interests of one class of funeral directors that some morticians act as if ministers are their worst competitors; and in some cases, they are right. For various reasons, such as a clear conviction about life after death, many pastors regard "mortal remains" as just that—what is left after one who was loved is no longer there. From this starting point, they attempt to turn the survivors' focus away from the dead body and toward the life that remains for them to live in this world. On the other hand, concentration on the connection between the body and the loved one who had lived in it, a subtle denial that "the deceased" is really dead, along with a sense of obligation to show love for the person by treating the body well—and, perhaps, atoning for past slights to the person by extravagant treatment of the body— is the attitude that leads to high-margin purchases of casket and funerary services. Profit-minded funeral directors do well to get a signature on a contract before the grieving survivor has a chance to talk to his or her pastor or priest. The mortuary business, or at least some of its most conspicuous practitioners, seems committed to denying and perverting the transition being discussed here. Even an experienced pastor would do well to take another pastor along when making arrangements in his or her bereavement with a funeral director.

After we die, of course, we are freed from concern over matters of this kind. During our living before dying, however, we can take steps to make the final rituals much easier for our loved ones. One way of doing this is visiting a mortuary and arranging a prepaid funeral for ourselves. Two things may hold us back from such a step: it may be hard to acknowledge our mortality in such a concrete way, and it may be hard to decide on such a significant expenditure—a decision that we (unlike our survivors) have the luxury of postponing. A clear recognition of the nature of these obstacles may be enough to allow us to overcome them. If not, we can seek help from the person or persons who will inherit the responsibility if we do not act. We can expect them to help, partly because they will be helping themselves at the same time, and more particularly because they are the people who love us and want to help us. Perhaps they will accompany us to the funeral parlor, or at least discuss the issue with us before we go, clarifying the choices and sharing the decisions. Choices between burial and cremation, whether or not to hold viewing hours, public funeral or a private funeral with a memorial service later, all present difficult decisions. They are much more easily made in advance when emotions are calmer and time-pressure is less intense than it will be in the hours immediately following death.

More than one friend of mine has overlooked an important decision in advance planning. The final disposal of ashes after cremation—home storage, vault, burial, or scattering (scattering where?)—often seems to surprise survivors carrying out the last wishes of a dead family member of friend. Different localities have different possibilities and restrictions relating to scattering human ashes, so advice is seldom useful unless it comes from local sources. The one step that is almost certainly helpful is to make the manner and place of disposal of the ashes a specific part of the discussion with family, friends, or counselor. Anyone who suggests a feasible means of disposal as a part of an expressed preference for cremation can greatly ease the burden of survivors.

Another way of dealing with the issue is through a funeral society, burial society, or other group with similar titles. These associations provide low-cost funerals on a prepaid basis, allowing you to bypass profit-motivated sales pressure almost entirely. Consumer guides, such as *The Yellow Pages*, frequently contain listings for such organizations. It is worth the effort to find one.

Members of Swedenborgian churches observe a variety of funeral practices. Their emphasis on the continuing life of a person's spirit leads Swedenborgians away from focusing on bodily remains and from concerns about funerary practices. In my acquaintance, many people choose cremation as the least troublesome among the options. Wakes are not part of the tradition; but open-casket visiting hours at the mortuary are common, as are gatherings of some kind—coffee, reception, dinner, or a large party (at home or at the church). A significant number of families opt for a private cremation or interment service, followed by a memorial service at a later date, and some hold a memorial service as their only public observation of the death.

Something of the Swedenborgian attitude toward dying appears in observations at annual general conventions of Swedenborgian churches. Current practice is to devote an early-morning celebration of the Holy Supper to memorializing ministers and prominent church leaders who have died during the year, with an opportunity to recall the names of all church members who died since the last convention. For many decades until the recent past, a memorial was read on the floor during business sessions for any minister or church officer who had died, and a period of silence was observed in his memory (only men were ordained in those days). One year the Council of Ministers discussed this practice and entertained the proposal that the moment of silence be replaced by a standing round of applause in celebration for the life of this person whom we loved. After some grumbling from ministers reluctant to change tradition, the motion was adopted as a trial practice. When the next ministerial death occurred, however, the man's widow expressed great distress at the prospect of applause greeting the announcement of her husband's death, so the idea was abandoned.

Eventually, of course, a funeral plan is arranged, and a mortician engaged. Then, the survivors reach a stage of the ritual that is outside the area of professional help. Whether there are viewing hours at a funeral home, people visiting the home of the deceased person, a wake (or similar occasion by another name, such as "reception"), or other arrangements, there is a time at which the survivors closest to the person who died meet other relatives and friends. This is when the spouse, or other close relation, recalls the details of the death for each visitor, telling the story again and again. Often, the frequent repetition sets the story into an unintentionally memorized routine. This act of the postmortem ritual has a long history and has been almost obligatory for many generations. It is a part that offended me when, as a young adult, I was centrally involved in a funeral for the first time. It seemed to me a totally unfair burden to impose on someone (my Aunt Alice, when her husband died, several years before she did) who had already been brought into a state of fragile emotions by the recent death. Time, experience, and especially reading accounts of the follow-up study after the Coconut Grove fire, have taught me to appreciate such ritual.

The Coconut Grove was a large Boston restaurant and

nightclub, which burned down on November 28, 1942, with many people killed in the fire and ensuing panic. Since it was unusual to find such a large group of survivors in close geographic proximity, a group of psychologists interviewed the survivors and follow-up interviews were made with the same group over a period of years. Professional journals and popular psychology magazines reported the findings, and one struck me with special force.

The original interviews revealed two general types among the survivors: one group grieved demonstrably, weeping, and repeating details of the tragedy several times during the interview. The other group was noticeably undemonstrative, speaking with relatively calm resignation of the overall tragedy and their personal loss. Interviews at intervals for twenty-five years or more showed that people in the undemonstrative group had received psychological or psychiatric treatment during the years at a rate much higher than average, while members of the demonstrative group sought such treatment at a rate slightly below average. Whether the results indicate that emotionally healthy people are more demonstrative about their feelings than repressed people or that ventilation of emotions aids psychic health may not be clear. But the study decisively indicates a positive correlation between demonstrative grieving (including repetition of details about the death event), and psychological health in the wake of serious disturbance. These data, together with my own later experience (which has been shaped to some extent by the Coconut Grove study), convince me that funerary rituals have significant spiritual and psychological values for the bereaved survivors.

One of the spiritual values of repeated, verbal, explicit descriptions of a loved one's death grows out of their reinforcing the acknowledgment of the fact and the finality of death. The spirit's continued living is independent of the body that dies, but it cannot overcome the body's inherent mortality. I have known bereaved Christians, unquestioningly certain that their loved one was living in a new way after dying, who felt guilty at having so strong a sense of loss and of grief. It is as though their knowledge of ongoing life was supposed to make them somehow superior to death, as if grieving were a kind of betrayal of their faith. It is not so. So long as we are human—inseparably physical and spiritual—death is part of our life. It is only our spirit, which will become independent of our body, of which we can say with the apostle Paul, "Death has no dominion" (Romans 6:9).

Grief ∽

The busy-ness, the obligations, the visitors, the weariness, and the aching emotional numbness of the period between the death and the funeral eventually are attended to or wear off. It is then, rather than at the time of the death, that survivors of a loved one's death must begin the serious work of grieving. For some time now, the process that people go through after bereavement has been called "grief work" in popular and professional literature on the subject. The term is useful. Grieving is more a job to be done than it is a burden to be borne. Grieving is work, a process that takes time, emotional effort, and spiritual energy to complete. It is a task with natural and predictable stages, a job for which you can get amateur help from friends or professional help from books or counselors. Grieving is a project that will change your outlook on life, your emotional strength, and your spiritual character—change them for the better, if you grieve well and fully.

This is not the place for a description of the predictable stages of normal grieving, nor for specific advice on how to do the work in the most effective and advantageous way. Excellent books on those subjects deal with the stages of grief in detail. A classic overview of the subject is Judith Viorst's *Necessary Losses: The Loves, Illusions, Dependencies, and Impossible Expectations That All of Us Have to Give Up in Order to Grow* (1986). This book is of most value to readers at some emotional distance from the experience of losing a loved one. Several shorter books can be recommended to people in the midst of coping with loss. New in the field is Brent Waters' compassionate little book *Dying and Death* (1996), a work aimed at congregations to help them help each other, although it is a resource for the individual mourner as well. Among other recent publications, one of the tenderest, most innovative, and most useful is *How to Survive the Loss of a Love* (1991) by Melba Colgrove, Harold H. Bloomfield, and Peter McWilliams. Finally, I'd recommend Earl A. Grollman's *Living When a Loved One Has Died* (1977) and Alla Renée Bozarth's *A Journey through Grief: Gentle, Specific Help to Get You through the Most Difficult Stages of Grieving* (1990).

Any of these books, or a combination of two or three, can be useful in the struggle to deal with the emotions and myriad thoughts that flood a person's consciousness in time of grief. Sessions with a social worker or therapist are valuable, if referrals are available to ward off having to make another decision. And simply talking with as many friends as possible, repeating the story, is particularly important. What needs emphasis here is the importance of grief work, its place in the transition between one kind of living and another, and its place in our preparation for our own coming transition. It is essential to prepare for grief and, when the period of mourning is at hand, not to avoid it or repress it.

Because no one dies without affecting others, and most affect one or a few with particular intensity, those most closely affected are part of the transition of the person who dies. The emotional pain of dying, for many people, involves the sense of breaking a relationship and leaving another behind. That pain is echoed in the pain of the bereaved. Certainty that the loved one will awake to new life in another realm may bring a kind of comfort to one side of the brain, one aspect of our personality. But joy for the loved one's new life does not diminish our loss of his or her presence with us—the sight, the touch, the kinds of physical and emotional support that are possible only in physical life. When the bond is very close, involving spiritual sharing as well as emotional and physical connections, a survivor's grief may affect the one who died, whose spirit is still alive. That possibility could explain the frequency with which visions of or messages from recently deceased loved ones are reported by grieving survivors. Such occurrences are discussed by Swedenborg in *Arcana Coelestia* 5726.

In the nineteenth century, major efforts were made in England and the United States to accumulate scientific documentation of appearances of this kind, attempting to document what F. W. H. Myers' monumental 1903 study called *Human Personality and Its Survival of Bodily Death*. The British Society for Psychical Research and its American counterpart compiled massive stores of such evidence, and the work was continued in the mid-twentieth century by J. B. Rhyne at Duke University. Recent research, like that of Mel Morse in *Parting Visions* (1994), demonstrates once again that many people experience visual and sometimes audible visitations from loved ones or close friends at the time of death. Despite attending elements of surprise and grief, these visits usually are remembered as reassuring or comforting.

In any event, the survivor's grieving is part of the event of the death of one who dies, not a separate, merely conse- quent, event. This means, among others, that attending pro- fessionals and all concerned need to regard the closest supporters/survivors as full participants in the event. Grief work usually begins before death, whether or not it is per- ceived by the survivors or the health-care professionals around them as grieving. In the "death scenes" discussed previously, survivors of all the deaths except some of the catastrophic events do a great deal of important and lasting grief work in the sick-room during the late stages of the pa- tient's affliction. Health-care professionals affect this process in many ways, only a few of which they can deliberately control and even fewer that are in their overloaded job de- scriptions. Their primary responsibility is care for the pa- tient, but the many levels of interconnection between the patient and the loving attendants at the bedside preclude any simple separation. Care for a dying patient includes care for those close to him or her, and care for the comforters comforts the patient.

The most valuable help for the comforter may well come from the hospice professionals. The "intake" worker, the caseworker, the nurse, the social worker, the technicians, aides, and other professionals from hospice give the attender or caretaker (who may feel close to the end of his or her rope by the time they are called) the feeling of a besieged outpost watching the rescuing cavalry charging over the hill. The sense of "we're here and it's all right; you can relax now" is enough to bring tears of relief.

The kind of care that loving attendants need varies widely with the case and the individual personalities involved. However, outside certain specialized nursing homes and the hospice movement, there are long-standing patterns of professional behavior that are obviously counterproductive when viewed from this perspective. Doctors' reluctance to discuss alternative treatment plans—including "no-treatment" options permitting natural death—excludes supporters from participation in decisions affecting their loved one's treatment and deprives them of the best information on which to be doing their grief work. It is standard care practice in many hospitals for nurses, aides, and technicians to ask visitors to leave the room during routine procedures. Such procedures often require two professionals to do what could be done by one in many cases with the willing and capable help of family members.

At the same time, health-care providers impede grief work by distorting the survivors' perception of their close involvement in the patient's process, whether of healing or dying. These and similar practices of physicians and nurses became common defenses against difficulties occasioned by visitors' attempting micromanagement of cases far beyond their training or emotional capacity, and by their interfering in bedside procedures. However, a general population with increased medical sophistication, and increasingly complex grief work to be done, needs more inclusive participation in "end game" practices of medical institutions than is customarily offered.

12 ❧
Angels, Ready and Able

While the preceding chapters may read like a laundry list of troubles faced by dying patients and their loving survivors, they are by no means a complete description of all the difficulties to be encountered. There may be significant satisfactions and some joy; for the most part they are not appreciated (or even recognized) until later. Overall, the process of severing the intricate links between human body and spirit usually is painful to endure, painful to watch and attend, painful even to think about. It might seem amazing that anyone dies quietly and peacefully, or that survivors find any satisfaction or joy in memories of the event.

Both of those things do happen. Maybe they do not happen often enough, but they are not rare. Much of the credit is due to health-care providers who serve the needs of patients and visitors with truly admirable skill and gentleness, despite a variety of institutional failings and occasional personal ones. Most hospice workers deserve special praise in this regard. Also, bedside attenders have more physical, mental, and spiritual strength and resources than they realize before they are tested. Finally, and far from least, there are other agents that help us all, even though they may not be visible, tangible, or vocal. These agents include angels and other spirits who help the dying and the surviving in many ways, some of which are the subject of this chapter.

Spiritual community ~

Every human being is a complex interaction between a body and a spirit. The spiritual element of this dynamic union can be conscious of its physical environment or its spiritual one, and in some circumstances becomes aware of both at one time. Even in the absence of conscious perceptions of one environment or the other, human personality is influenced continually by both realities. In deep mental concentration or spiritual meditation, for instance, the mind blocks out most awareness of the body's environmental temperature. The physical body chills just the same, even if we don't notice when the ambient temperature drops. The subconscious mind monitors the change until at some point it intrudes into the conscious mind with a message that it is time to get a sweater. Similarly, when the mind becomes preoccupied with physical details of caring for a patient at home or juggling schedules to allow time with a patient in the hospital, spiritual guidance, support, or comfort presses upon the subconscious mind, sometimes breaking into consciousness when a particular realization or feeling is particularly needed.

At the same time that it is connected to its physical body, and thus with a physical community, each human spirit is connected with a spiritual community, even though we normally are not consciously aware of the latter connection. This interconnectedness is essential to spiritual life and wellbeing. Breaking the familiar kinds of connections with a physical community is part of the pain of death—pain to the dying person and pain to the broken family and close friends. Spiritual connections are not limited by physical time or space, so even the hypothetical person "alone on a desert island" continues to be in a spiritual community, and through that community is connected to all of reality—particularly with the source of all being, living, discerning, and intending: God.

From that perspective, we are never alone, no matter how isolated we may feel ourselves to be. Even the feeling of isolation is a consequence of our turning our backs on our spiritual community, rather than our community's withdrawal from us. It is during the difficult and lonely times of bedside vigils, that spirits in the communities of the patient and the watchers help everyone involved, in a variety of ways.

Our consciousness of such involvement may be induced by prayer, Bible-reading, or even fragmentary recollection of poems or songs. In my experience, prayer has been my best ally when struggling with anxiety and the sense of isolation from help or support. Sometimes it is difficult to acknowledge my fears to a friend or even (perhaps especially!) to family, and untrained advice often sounds as though I'm being counseled to deny or repress my feelings. But I can confess anything in prayer, and praying for help has actually changed the way I feel. One way of understanding such change: by asking the Lord for help, I separate my "self" (my spirit) from spirits with worldly focuses and self-centered motivations, and associate my self with those who are accustomed to turning to God and to offering spiritual help. Also, perhaps more directly, the Lord uses my spiritual companions' influence on me to answer my prayers.

I also have found help by contemplating certain biblical passages. Bibles are often available when needed: most

people have one at home and the Gideons have placed
them in many hospitals rooms and hotels where people stay
while keeping hospital vigils. I have been helped by many
of the Psalms. A few that have been most comforting are
listed below:

∾

Psalm 13: "How long, O Lord? Wilt thou forget me
forever?"
Psalm 23: "The Lord is my shepherd; I shall not want."
Psalm 46: "God is our refuge and strength, a very present
help in trouble."
Psalm 121: "I lift up my eyes to the hills."
Psalm 130: "Out of the depths, I cry to thee, O Lord!"
Psalm 139: O Lord, thou hast searched me and known
me."

∾

After the book of Psalms, my most fruitful searches have
been in the Gospels. Almost all the stories and the sayings
of Jesus are comforting in some way. My personal favorites
are clustered in the gospel of John:

∾

- picturing myself coming to the Lord in the darkness of
my night (3:1-21);
- imagining Jesus weeping with me as he did for
Lazarus, Mary, and Martha (11);
- accepting the promises found in John 14 and 15.

∾

In other gospels, I have found it helpful to recall Jesus'
promise of rest for all who come to him (Matthew 11:28-
30); identify my distress with the woman's hemorrhaging

(Mark 7:24-30); and trust the promise found in Luke (12:4-7). Random searching through the Psalms and the Gospels uncovers passages that are helpful to anyone seeking spiritual solace.

The spirit of the dying patient has been involved with its spiritual community all along and will come into full participation in it as soon as separation from the body is complete. As the transition approaches, other members of the community become more clearly conscious of him or her, interacting more intentionally than before. In this way, preparation begins for his or her welcome to the new way of living, so the fellowship that seems new and strange to the awakening spirit also feels somehow familiar, like home. People who advance to old age, particularly if they have recognized and developed their spiritual faculties, sometimes sense this transition. A few come to feel less at home in their physical environment than in their spiritual one.

This feeling of process was put into words most gracefully by a Swedenborgian minister, Chauncy Giles, shortly after the Civil War. But his experience was not unique. Something my Aunt June said during a visit in her advanced years (while she was still in good health) prompted me to copy a letter and some diary entries that Giles had written, and send them to her. She found them to be accurate descriptions and satisfying explanations of her own thoughts and experiences.

Giles wrote the following paragraph in a letter dated March 11, 1886, when he was 73 years old:

❧

The thought has frequently come to me lately that sickness and the growing infirmities of age are a gradual death, and it is pleasant and beautiful to think of them in this light. They are a gradual loosening of the bonds that bind body and spirit together. The loss of natural memory is the beginning of the process, which ends when we leave the body in being entirely closed, so that in our customary states of life in the spiritual world we have no recollection of this world and our life in it. By such gentle process does the Lord effect the great changes in our life.[7]

∽

This perspective is highly compatible with my observations of my wife, through the last stages of her illness. Our thirteen-year-old granddaughter said of her, "It seems like Grandma will be in heaven already by the time she's dead."

Celestial helpers and spiritual guides ∽

In life's major crises, physical death being a preeminent example, help is available from beyond the patient's primary spiritual community. According to Swedenborg, angels who are endowed with special affections and skills and commissioned with special powers gather to help the spirit whose body is dying prepare for the transition to fully spiritual living. Patients who are open to angelic influence and can accept it without compromising their freedom sometimes are seen or heard responding to angels who have come to comfort and to welcome them. Even when there is no observable response, there may be an inexplicable change, such as a peaceful quietness after a period of intense agitation or apparent pain; or a sleeping countenance may change from frowning to semi-smiling as a result of angelic ministrations.

---

7. Carrie Giles Carter, *The Life of Chauncy Giles* (Boston: Massachusetts New-Church Union, 1920), 367.

Accounts of near-death experiences usually include a description of a being of light, an angel, or an exceptionally kind and beautiful person (three common forms of angelic appearance) who greets, guides, and explains things in the close approach to physical death. Similar appearances, usually in less dramatic scenes, have been reported by critically ill patients after sleeping or when waking from a coma. People who cannot accept angelic presence as easily have other kinds of experience with similar effects.

Angels in Action, a book I wrote previously, records the story of a close friend and colleague who died of a massive heart attack. Lying unconscious on the floor while the paramedics were on their way, my friend spoke without appearing to regain consciousness: "Yes, I understand what you're trying to do." I have always believed that he was speaking to angels who were helping him prepare for the imminent separation from his body. For people in the process of scheduled dying, awareness of spiritual presence and assistance often begins long before the actual moment of death. One effect of this aid is the tranquility that precedes death for some patients. I recall, for example, my Aunt June's disregard for bedsores, the calmness of my father—conscious enough to squeeze my hand, yet relaxed in spite of his labored breathing—and other friends and friends of friends who died quietly. If they did not die with all the dignity we might hope for them, at least they died in peace. I cannot doubt that peace is more valuable to one's spirit than earthly visions of dignity. And angels help us achieve what we *really* need.

Family members or friends, involved with the death of a loved one by caring and by watching, are members of their own spiritual communities, with their own spiritual guides and supporters. Spouses who have lived together long and lovingly enough to approach what Swedenborg calls a "truly conjugial" relationship may be part of the same spiritual community and receive help from the same or similar sources. In both kinds of situations, different kinds of spiritual help are needed by the watchers than by the patient, so the experience is different. Surviving spouses need to prepare for ongoing physical living in a physical environment that is significantly changed by the loss of a loved one. One aspect of such preparation may be new or renewed realizations about the reality of continuing life, so that sorrow at loss of the loved one may be balanced by joy at his or her freedom from pain and disability, as well as the promise of a future reunion. I have mentioned my wife's mother expecting to join her own mother as soon as she "returned home"; and my friend who saw her husband at the foot of her bed, waiting for her to join him. A friend of mine whose wife died a little more than a year ago told me last summer of his activity with friends and a new hobby, flying lessons (which his wife had been afraid for him to take while she lived), which shows him living strongly in the present. However, several clues in his conversation suggest to me that everything he does is part of his preparation for getting on with the *real* rest of his life just as soon as his present good health abandons him and allows him to rejoin her. When a loving survivor understands that a spiritual reunion with the beloved awaits, the feeling of loss can be alleviated.

13 ∽
Awakening from Death

The process by which a spirit separates itself from its physical body involves the most essential aspects of our human nature and the reality in which we live, including the kinds of connections that bind our body to our spirit in the first place. Swedenborg describes these connections in passages scattered between early chapters of *Arcana Coelestia*; these passages have been compiled by George F. Dole in his recent translation of Swedenborg's *The Universal Human and Soul-Body Interaction* (1984).

In general terms, these connections are part of the structure of all creation and involve spiritual purposes and energy being ultimately grounded in the functions of human organs and body parts. For example, the function of true perceptions and ideas—clarifying intentions and preparing them for accomplishment—is connected to the pulmonary function of the lungs, which cleanses and aerates the blood in preparing it for another recirculating cycle. The spiritual function of true thoughts is related to the physical function of the pulmonary process as an electrical charge is related to its ground. Parallel relationships are integral to every specific individual thing that exists, connecting spiritual reality to physical objects in an overall structure that Swedenborg has called "correspondences."

The energy or life force of a spirit is love (or our true intention), and this is grounded in the heart's activity, which circulates the blood prepared by the lungs, thus sustaining physical life. When these connections with the heart's and lungs' spiritual taproots are broken, there are two interconnected reactions: the physical body loses its ability to support its spirit, and the sundered correspondence frees the spirit from its body. This cessation of bodily function—cardiopulmonary activity—deprives the body of its spirit, and the broken correspondence severs the spirit from the body.

Death entails the severing of both bonds. When cardiac function continues for a while after breathing has stopped, the spirit remains in the body for that period. We have no witness comparable to Swedenborg's regarding modern questions about "brain death"; but there is no evidence of meaningful electro-encephalic activity after the cessation of cardiac functioning. When both breath and heartbeat have stopped, the spirit may feel what Swedenborg described as a sensation of being "drawn" from the body, and separation becomes complete.

Losing our physical senses usually includes our spirit's losing consciousness. Waking to purely spiritual awareness is carefully managed and assisted to avoid or minimize shock or fear or other difficulty. Ordinarily, this "sleep of death"— as Hamlet called it—ends gradually. Our first consciousness, before we open our eyes to our whole environment, is a dream-like awareness of kind and comforting faces close to our own. They do not speak, but their expressions communicate clearly that everything is all right, and we will be cared for because we are among friends. These faces are the faces of celestial angels, angels from high in the heavens where love is supreme over understanding. They are so different from the physical people we have been associating with until now that we could not understand a word they said if they were to speak and would have great trouble looking at the brightness around them if we were to open our eyes; but we are able to know their thoughts and be comforted by their concern for us.

When we recognize and accept their message of comfort, they help us understand what might otherwise be frightening, as our spirit is being pulled—almost sensibly—from our body. At this point, the spirits who had been around us as we were dying realize that the physical-spiritual person they had known is dead and move away to other interests. The celestial angels guard us and reassure us until they are replaced by other angels, spiritual angels who are not so radically different from our own spirit.

The first thing these angels do is open our spiritual eyes. It is as if they pull a veil or cover from our eyes, beginning in the corner of the left eye and moving toward the bridge of the nose, so that we can see. At first, we only see brightness, but gradually we make out colors and shapes. Then, as if another covering were lifted from our face, we can see all our surroundings. This is the beginning of spiritual thought. Since it possible for us to understand them now, the angels tell us that our body has died, and we are now a spirit.

A man or woman who has not been expecting death in the foreseeable future may not have formed any kind of strong expectation beyond the point of dying. But whether continued living is a surprise or not, the sudden nature of the transition sometimes creates a problem. For various possible reasons, such as if fear and pain had been suppressed below consciousness in the final moments of physical life, there may at first be no awareness of having died. In such a case, the spirit may awake in new surroundings in the same way people normally begin a dream experience unaware at first that there is anything unusual about the situation or that it is radically discontinuous from the previous moment of consciousness. Therefore, the first task of angels greeting the spirit into the realm of purely spiritual living sometimes is to communicate in a loving and reassuring way that his or her physical body has died. This news is accepted somewhat more easily by newly awakened spirits who had expected to find themselves living in some way after dying than by those who anticipated oblivion; but angels manage the job no matter what the case.

For many people sudden death disrupts the spirit's goals and expectations. If dying had been caused, for example, by driving too fast in an effort to keep an appointment, the spirit may be still anxious about keeping it or about accomplishing the purpose of the scheduled meeting. Such anxieties and the goals related to them are changed by the shift in perspective that accompanies the transition to spiritual living, as mystics and other wise people have long urged their companions to realize. The goal that was being pursued is revalued from the spiritual point of view, which spirits gain when they lose their bodies. New ways of accomplishing things may also may appear. The importance and relevance to their new life diminishes as new companions and activities attract their attention. Most activities of our physical life have spiritual implication; and it is conceivable that spirits would continue working on these ramifications after dying.

On the other hand, unexpected dying can be premature, in the sense of occurring before a person's character has fully developed a consistent pattern of values and intentions. This is most obvious when infants die, but it also is true of older children and of immature young adults. Since it may seem that we grow tall, grow strong, grow set in our ways, and even grow old, before we ever grow up, this might appear to be almost the universal situation. It is not, however: purposes and perspectives harden into an adult personality without any outward sign of their maturity or their nature. They are apparent only to spiritual vision.

Those who die before forming a recognizable life's love complete their maturation in the spiritual world. Since their mentors and role models then are angels, whatever sort of people had guided them during physical life, they tend to become angelic as they grow. Infants, who had no opportunities to adopt any sinful inclinations, grow into angels of particular purity and beauty, advancing to handsome young adulthood and remaining in that state for eternity. They remain distinguishable from angels who overcame evil inclinations and formed a good character out of struggles against temptations during physical living. Angels of this latter kind can be recognized by the physical affections that remain in the external aspects of their actions and appearance, as Swedenborg relates in *Heaven and Hell* 349. And in a converse fashion, just as infants progress in spiritual beauty to a handsome adulthood, people who lived to an advanced age are seen in the spiritual world to develop toward the appearance of the prime of life. "To grow old in heaven," Swedenborg says in *Heaven and Hell* 414, "is to grow young."

Since dying unexpectedly is significantly more common among people younger than fifty years old than among older people, this kind of transition to living beyond dying usually leads to a slower discovery of their real character. This means that such spirits take longer to find and accept their home and their home community. People who die at older ages typically have more opportunity and more incentive to review and evaluate their lives in the honesty that can be rooted in introspection. Those who undertake this process, and actually are capable of being honest with themselves, may have much less that is new to discover in purely spiritual living, fewer adjustments to make, and so need less "time" (that is, needing fewer changes of their self-understanding) to find and recognize their place in the spiritual universe. Victims of sudden death may need more. Whatever is needed is provided, however, for God manages our lives in such a way that everyone dies "on time" from a spiritual perspective.

The ensuing processes of becoming familiar with spiritual surroundings and finding our spiritual home were described in Part I. What is important to notice about the transition from our past life of the body to our new life of the spirit is the gentle calm that pervades it. Whether the process of dying was prolonged or sudden, peaceful or violent, easy or painful, the process of waking to new living is as comfortable as heaven's angels can make it.

Epilogue ∽

I n the earlier section on grief, I noted that close sup-porters/survivors participate significantly in the death event along with the patient. To a person who has lost a deeply loved spouse, partner, friend, child, or other family member, there can be comfort in the picture of the loved one starting a new stage of life under loving care in beautiful surroundings; but the same picture can bring a sharp stab of lonely pain as well. I have sat with friends who felt that pain, and I have felt it myself.

As I write these words, it has been less than a year since my wife's death, described in the introduction; so it is obvi-ously too early for me to testify to the full experience of survival. After only a few months, however, some things al-ready are clear and worth sharing.

For one thing, I have realized that my loss is not some-thing to "recover from" or to "get over." The pain of griev-ing does ease somewhat, and intense grief that overwhelms my consciousness becomes more transitory and less fre-quent. But my recovery of the ability to function—to feel energy in place of numb inertia, to accomplish simple tasks when I set out to do them—and to experience pleasure and happiness has been helped by recognizing Marian's continu-ing influence in my life. Although I am physically alone, I am the man she lived with for forty-eight years, and she is very much a part of the person I have become in that time. I enjoy doing things that I remember she liked to have me do, although pain still is mixed with pleasure when I do things we often enjoyed doing together. The furniture and decorations in my home are things we chose together, so I feel that I am living in *our* place, rather than simply in *my* place.

In chapter 2, I referred to Swedenborg's report that couples in a "truly marital" relationship are only partially separated by the death of one partner. He speaks here of more than the kind of abiding and sustaining memories I just mentioned:

∾

[Couples who] were united as to souls and thence as to minds (this unition being spiritual) are not separated by the death of one of them. The spirit of the deceased partner dwells continually with the spirit of the one not yet deceased, and this until the death of the latter, when they meet again and reunite and love each other more tenderly than before because [they are] in the spiritual world.

Conjugial Love 321

∾

What this means in my life is not yet entirely clear. The state of my spiritual union, like the state of my spiritual regeneration, is hard to judge for myself, so I cannot yet be certain how the promise applies to me. Further, I am uncertain what it is or would be like, exactly, to have Marian's spirit "dwelling continually" with me. I *am* sure that phrase describes a kind of relationship or presence that does not intrude on my freedom of choice or my normal life. Twice in nine months, I have dreamt of seeing her face break into a happy smile; once I felt her warn me in time to avoid an impending car accident at freeway speed; and some of those times I felt helped by memories of her seemed to have been spiritual influence. These may be signs or symptoms of her on-going presence in *our* apartment. In any case, the promise and these experiences do not have to *prove* anything to make me feel good!

A third observation from my brief experience as a survivor involves a "chicken-and-egg" problem that arises in various kinds of crises, including learning to live with great loss. When I feel good, I am more active and more inclined to get on with life; and when I'm active and busy, I feel better. The ups and downs of recent months have taught me beyond any doubt that the road to adjustment and new life follows the second formula rather than the first. Moving my muscles and challenging my mind gets me out of the depressive lethargy that floods in when grief is spent, and helps me feel better physically, mentally, and spiritually. Waiting to feel better before getting active is like waiting on the street corner for a parade that is going down another street.

While I do not seek recovery from my loss, I do pray for—and work toward—recovery from the despondency with which I first reacted to loss. The pain does ease, the memories help more than they hurt, I have help from my spiritual community (which includes my wife whose body alone died), and activity breeds energy for more activity in a healthy spiral of living. For patient and survivor alike, living really does continue after dying.

Rev. Robert H. Kirven
8650   Apt. 316
North 65th Street
Glendale, Arizona, 85302